generative
scribing

generative
scribing

A SOCIAL ART
of the 21st CENTURY

Kelvy Bird

PI PRESS
Cambridge, Massachusetts

PI Press
Presencing Institute
1770 Massachusetts Avenue
Cambridge, MA 02140 USA
press@presencing.com

ISBN: 978-0-9997179-9-8

First Edition, Second Printing

Book design by Thais Erre Felix in collaboration with Ricardo Gonçalves.
All art and photographs by Kelvy Bird, unless otherwise noted.

For larger, digital versions of the images in the appendix, visit: www.kelvybird.com.

for all who aspire to see

contents

foreword

In *The Birth of Tragedy*, Nietzsche suggests that his task as
a philosopher was to "look at science through the optic of
the artist, and to look at art through the optic of life." Kelvy
Bird's book does in the world of scribing and social art what
Nietzsche's work did in the world of philosophy: it marks the
end of one period and foreshadows the beginning of another.

I have known Kelvy for more than twenty years, as a
client (I employed her to scribe during client engagements),
as a colleague (we co-created the Presencing Institute),
and as a friend. Having also worked with many other scribe
practitioners over the years, I have a good sense of how
significant the body of work is that Kelvy, together with
her colleagues, has developed.

I have seen Kelvy grow from a remarkable scribe practitioner
to a true pioneer of an entirely new quality of scribing.
In her work, Kelvy translates ideas, concepts, and processes
into imagery by listening from a deeper place, what I call the
Source. The goal is to make this Source level of awareness
more accessible, in order to "presence" what a group or a social
system wants to express, and then make it visible.

Accomplishing this is at the heart of this book. It's not a linear
process. It's an attunement to a field. It's the art of allowing
your hand to move and operate *from* the field, expressing the
collective knowing, the felt sense in a system or group.
How do you do that? By opening your heart. And when you
are lucky, you connect to the collective by opening their hearts
too. The result is a visualization of collective footprints that
functions as a mirror that groups can use to look at their work
and their journeys from a new angle.

That is the territory that this book investigates and explores
as an emerging discipline. It's relevant not only to scribe
practitioners who want to evolve their practice to do

generative scribing. It is also relevant for other social artists, facilitators, and presencing practitioners who want to hone their capacity to activate generative social fields.

When I read the "Model of Practice" section of the book, it struck me that Kelvy's integrative drawing actually looks and works like an upside-down human being: with the open mind at the bottom (knowing), the open heart at the center (being, perceiving, joining), and the open will at the top (drawing). The process that Kelvy describes starts at the heart, continues with the action, and then results in new knowledge. So it's the opposite of conventional wisdom, which has us operating from the head to the hand (usually ignoring the heart).

Over the years I have seen Kelvy's drawings transform from capturing a lot to capturing only the essence. The more focused the drawing, the more powerful its impact on me and on a group. Capturing the essence of an idea requires courage to leave things out (to let go). When I see the impact of her drawings on a group, her skill is very visibly validated. I have also learned that, as a facilitator, if I hand the microphone to Kelvy mid-process and at the end—she often captures the deeper tonality and feeling of the field better than anyone else. As a consequence, today, when facilitating, I partner with scribes not only so that they capture what's being said, but in order to jointly activate a generative social field.

It has been said of Michelangelo that everything he touched was transformed by beauty. In collaborating and co-creating with Kelvy it has been my experience that the same can be said about the social fields she touches. Scribing is a social art that no one can practice alone. It requires inner cultivation and refinement, which Kelvy has mastered. This book is a guide to this deeper territory. Enjoy!

—C. Otto Scharmer

acknowledgments

I open this space of thanks with unwavering love for my brother, Matthew Bird. Yes, he contributed 452 comments on draft 7a. But more enduring than fleeting edits is our shared way of approaching possibility. Recently, during the solar eclipse, we went to Walden Pond for a picnic. At one point we decided to take a swim. After venturing almost halfway across the body of water, I turned around, saw Matthew watching, and decided to break through my fear to keep going. I made it to the other side, raising my arms in triumph. My brother, faintly visible, raised his arms as well. One dot, alone; two dots, a line.

Thanks to my mom, Judith Nichtern, who once went out on a limb to paint a fifty-foot-high mural in a mall, and who has repeatedly modeled risk-taking and courage. Thanks to my dad, Harry Bird, who would use a toothpick to carve elaborate scenes into mushrooms from the woods, infusing in me a spirit of curiosity to seek delight in unexpected ways and places. Each seeded my core creativity from an early age.

To all the participants in the workshops I've co-delivered— and for the shared development of this material over years with dear colleagues Aaron Williamson, Alicia Bramlett, Alfredo Carlo, Angela Baldini, Bryan Coffman, Christopher Fuller, Dan Newman, Jayce Pei Yu Lee, Julie Arts, Lili Xu, Lucia Fabiani, Marga Biller, Mike Fleisch, Nico Gros, Peter Durand, Ripley Lin, Robert Hanig, Sita Magnuson, Svenja Rüger, and others—I thank you with a thousand snaps for your conversations and encouragement along the way.

A deep bow of gratitude goes to the team that helped me through key stages of the writing with their generous support and insight: Aimee Aubin, Brian Jones, Jane Lewis, Nadia Colburn, Robert Smyth, and Tamar Harel. And to JJP for endless patience and space, as well as incredible steadiness.

Janet Mowery provided absolutely critical copy editing and overall fine-tuning. Her guidance was essential in the final leg of production, and I extend my deepest thanks for her help. Thais Erre Felix created the beautiful cover and page design.

Much appreciation goes to all of my old friends in Consensus, the MG Taylor network, the ASE, Dialogos, the Value Web, dpict, and the Presencing Institute, and to newer friends in u.lab—what an adventure it has been and will continue to be.

To Eleanore Mikus, who taught me to consider the full frame of a picture, and to Barbara Cecil, Beth Jandernoa, Dorian Baroni, Glennifer Gillespie, and Peri Chickering, who opened my eyes to inner wholeness. I will be forever grateful for the mentorship of these remarkable women.

I have learned the power of restraint from Peter Senge, who has reinforced my—and the profession's—development for many years. We all can thank him!

Katrin Kaeufer's enthusiasm and genuine caring have consistently buoyed me through the ups and downs of this long process. Not only is the book more personal because of her input, its existence in print is largely due to her partnership.

And Otto Scharmer has championed the potential of generative scribing from the very beginning, with the foresight of a farmer who knows his soil and the talent of an astronomer who can map the stars. All creative acts root and stretch between these realms. Such has been, and continues to be, our collaboration.

Lastly, for every person who picks up this slim volume, I harbor a wide, welcoming smile for your interest in sharing some time here, together.

introduction

Each of our gestures, scribed on a wall or enacted in daily life, matters to the preservation and evolution of our species.

Scribing, one form of gesture, is a visual practice. An artist maps out ideas while people talk, and they can see a picture unfold right in front of their eyes. The drawing establishes connections within content, aids with insight, and supports decision-making. It's essentially a language that weaves words and pictures to facilitate group learning and cultural memory.

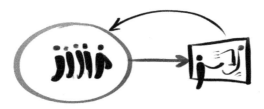

"Generative scribing" advances this discipline by extending the range of the practitioner to an entire ecosystem, while drawing with an attunement to energy. A generative scribe calls particular attention to an emerging reality that is brought to life by, and for, the social field in which it's created. No picture exists outside the context of the system in conversation, and the system's comprehension of itself is incomplete without the reflective representation and aid that the picture offers. It's a participatory, reciprocal, and procreative relationship.

Generative scribing is a visual practice unique in our age, a distinct art form of the 21st century, functioning in the moment, across cultural boundaries, and as a device for social seeing.

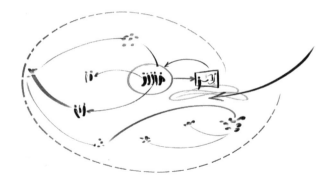

Because of its interactive and co-creative nature, generative scribing offers one access route to a sacred way of being, where the spirit of our humanity prevails over any individual agenda. Like witnesses of a solar eclipse at a pond, who share each other's special eyeglasses and swim together in muted waters, our spirits have an opportunity to revive and see anew because of common context. Drawing live, amongst a group of people, scribes make the human condition visible, tangible, known. In a way, we provide a setting, like a pond, for insight to occur.

But wait, what is the story behind scribing?

Scribing is a contemporary visual practice with roots in the Bay Area of California in the early 1970s. It is often defined as a practice that makes the unknown manifest through pictures, maps, diagrams, and models.[1] David Sibbet, founder of The Grove Consultants International, originated the terms "Group Graphics®" and the generic term "graphic facilitation" to describe methods that use visuals interactively to facilitate group understanding in organizational contexts.[2]

1   Robert Horn, "Visual Language and Converging Technologies in the Next 10–15 Years (and Beyond)," Paper prepared for the National Science Foundation Conference on Converging Technologies, December 2001.

2   David Sibbet, "A Graphic Facilitation Retrospective," http:// davidsibbet.com/wp-content/uploads/2016/12/ GF-RetrospectiveUpdated.pdf.

There are many cousins of scribing, each of which slightly varies the live drawing approach. One is "graphic recording," often a more literal means of pairing words and pictures, with an aim to mirror and map content. Other offshoots of the original practice have now-familiar terms such as sketchnoting, doodling, and mind mapping, to name a few —and all have found unique uses, markets, and applications. And I'd be remiss to omit the intersection with animation, motion graphics, cartooning, and even virtual reality, which have added dimensionality and access to the core profession in mind-boggling numbers.[3]

Practitioners in this field have come to learn the work in clear generational waves that I name in this manner:

1. **1970s: 1st Wave Originators** – like Sibbet, Jennifer Landau, and founding members of Grove Consultants along with Michael Doyle of Interaction Associates. (California, USA)

2. **1980s: 2nd Wave Originators** – Jim Channon, Matt Taylor, and Bryan Coffman with MG Taylor Corporation. (Colorado, USA)

3. **1990s: 3rd Wave Early Adopters** – those who learned with the originators and helped further seed the field (USA), those who started applying the practice within management consulting, organizational change, and not-for-profits. (+Canada, Europe)

4. **2000s: 4th Wave Early Majority** – those still learning from the previous generations in a hands-on manner, employing markers and physical wall surface and also starting to incorporate digital technologies. (+Australia)

3   Andrew Park, the extremely talented founder of Cognitive, invented the now ubiquitous whiteboard animation method, most widely known through the RSA Animate series that has received millions of views on YouTube. See the Cognitive website: www.wearecognitive.com.

5. **2010s: 5th Wave Self-Directed Majority** – people learning about the practice on their own, from books and videos by those who came up in the first four waves. (+Central and South America, Middle East, India, Africa, Asia)

6. **2017– : 6th Wave Collaborative Majority, Innovators, Questers** – people crossing regional boundaries to share best practices and evolve the art form; weaving indigenous, wisdom, and spiritual traditions into the existing visual practices to raise consciousness around the path of human evolution.

According to one of my earliest mentors, Bryan Coffman, the current use of the term "scribing" goes back at least as far as 1981, when knowledge workers who drew on walls during collaborative sessions were called "wall scribes."[4] As he once shared, "Scribes in Egypt kept the real story of what happened. Their word for the role was *Sesh*."[5]

According to Wikipedia, Seshat was the goddess of wisdom, knowledge, and credited with inventing writing. "Usually, she is shown holding a palm stem, bearing notches to denote the recording of the passage of time ... She was also depicted holding other tools and, often, holding the knotted cords that were stretched to survey land and structures."

I find this fascinating, considering that the current role of the scribe layers directly onto the original meaning. We mark the passage of time and delineate structure within, and for, cultures—albeit with new methods. Each drawing maps some

---

4   "Wall Scribing: One or two Graphics Team members listen to the conversation and draw what they hear. This is a form of instant feedback and visual translation for participants." *DesignShop Staff Manual, Athenaeum International, Version 3.3* (Boulder: MG Taylor Corporation, 1991), p. 37.

5   Donald Frazer, *Hieroglyphs and Arithmetic of the Ancient Egyptian Scribes: Version 1.* "The profession at first associated with the goddess Seshat is the source of the Egyptian word 'Sesh,' meaning scribe."

territory we are helping a social body to understand, whether it be a company's business strategy, a city's public land development, or a family's move to a new country.

Prehistoric cave paintings also served to record and chart the presence and activity of species. Native American medicine wheels, Tibetan Buddhist sand mandalas, and the dreamtime influence in Aboriginal art—along with many other ancient and contemporary co-created visual formats—include a spiritual approach to social art, recognizing the connection between humans and the life force all around us.

I have gravitated to the term "scribe" to define what I am and do because of this harkening back to something primordial, something that seems timeless and lasting, something that provides a service that cuts across any one lifetime.

Scribes serve as artistic aids in shared seeing and human navigation.

Scribes represent information, in as neutral a way as possible, to craft living artifacts. We draw, then document the work digitally, then let go of the original pieces by handing them off to clients; and sometimes we even wipe down our work surfaces immediately after a group ends their conversation.

The process is fleeting. The final digital images end up on people's smartphones, in documents, reprinted as posters, in reports, in library displays, and as handouts for those not in the room during the actual making of the piece.

But the physical artifact is a mere echo of the primary value, which is in-the-moment collective sourcing and reflection. In the process of making these artifacts, a group can see a course to take, find their direction. Thus the aid of the scribe is to induce greater vision, toward action.

Scribing is an inherently participatory social art form.

The painter Wassily Kandinsky viewed art as a liberating device that could bring the inner life alive through pure line, shape, and color.[6] Scribing, going beyond an abstract two-dimensional plane, activates the inner life of the social field, the unseen —yet felt—territory of human interaction.

Historically, two-dimensional art making has been a private, sheltered, creative act. Artists paint pictures, usually alone in a studio, based on their reality. Sometimes the pictures are exhibited, purchased, displayed in a home or public setting, and viewed. Sometimes they prompt conversation.

Scribing, as a social art, is an exposed, witnessed, feedback-dependent activity that only takes place within a group of people. It gives shape to human conditions in an organic way, in rhythm with what wants to be voiced and seen. It depends not on one artist's view, but on the input of many views that come together through the creative act.

When I work at a wall with a participant-audience at my back, the engagement is with both their content and their energy.[7] By responding to what I am hearing and sensing in an immediate way, live, in front of a group, what I create can be quickly assimilated into the conversation. Thus, through its reflective mirroring, the drawing has the power to immediately influence and transform the thinking in a room.

6   Wassily Kandinsky, *Concerning the Spiritual in Art* (London: Dover Publications, 1977), republished from the original *The Art of Spiritual Harmony* (London: Constable and Company Limited, 1914).

7   I often refer to those engaging with artwork as a "participant-audience" to intentionally help people think about an audience not as passive receivers of an artist's expression but as active players in the artwork's creation.

There is a reinforcing loop between the actual drawing and the receiving of the drawing; the loop expands the understanding that a room of people share and thereby expands their sense of possibility. (See appendix Figure 1.)

This art has life only because a communal desire for sensemaking exists. Someone, or a team, has decided to bring in a scribe to help people see what it is they are talking about.

What takes form through the hand of the scribe is the content that's meant to come through, no more and no less. What lands on a surface—no matter how well thought-through—is as far as a system can go at that moment. It reflects a slice of time.

Sailors cut through fog at a speed that allows them to hear the gonging buoys guiding their way. Chiropractors adjust a neck within the limits of the person's vertebral mobility. We can only move as fast as conditions allow, within a range of readiness. Scribes attune to those limits and track that movement.

I listen. I draw. You see. You speak. I listen I draw you see you speak. You see I listen you speak I draw. You speak I draw we see we listen. That's how it feels. It's fluid.

Scribing offers a relational way of seeing.

In 1933, color theorist Josef Albers arrived at Black Mountain College in North Carolina knowing few English words, but enough to convey his purpose for teaching: "To open eyes." [8]

My own inquiry into the relatedness of things began in earnest when reading and applying Albers's seminal book, *Interaction of Color*, during a university class called "Color, Form & Space." Professor Norman Daly challenged us: "Prove color is not independent." Through one homework assignment—placing two equivalent colors each within a different, larger, colored area—my eyes and mind were blown open by the very same grey appearing purple against yellow, then green against red.

As a painter, I started to attune to the relationships of color and objects everywhere. Beige against indigo: a moth, pinned against a screen, in darkness, seeking light. The inquiry extended to non-material things, too. Ideas side-by-side (my view, your view) . . . how to represent those juxtapositions? People side-by-side (my body heat, your body heat) . . . how to convey the vibrational field?

Then, in 1995, when working on a collaborative art project in San Francisco, I was introduced to scribing through Matt and Gail Taylor—an architect and an educator who developed a methodology for employing group genius in solving complex problems.[9] They invited me to apprentice at a DesignShop™ for NASA, a collaborative, immersive, three-day program to reimagine the use of wind tunnels. Most of what I remember

8 *Leap Before You Look: Black Mountain College, 1933–1957*, exhibit at the Institute of Contemporary Art, Boston, MA, October 2015–January 2016.

9 Gayle Pergamit and Chris Peterson, *Leaping the Abyss: Putting Group Genius to Work* (Hilton Head: knOwhere Press, 1997).

about that week is the impressive team of a dozen people that largely self-organized to facilitate over a hundred anxious and eager government employees of all ranks by arranging space, setting chairs, writing assignments, providing information, explaining concepts, documenting, filming, playing music —and yes, scribing! And, I recall being amazed at how art could have a role in shaping group thinking.

The environment itself extended my fascination with relation: over three days, participants wrote and drew out their concepts onto 6 x 8 foot rolling dry-erase walls, making thinking visible to everyone in the room. Through the placement of these large walls side-by-side, each containing ideas unique to individuals or breakout groups, suddenly I saw a format that extended my study of color into team dynamics.

I saw a way of representing multiple ideas from multiple people in one place, to stimulate overarching awareness and insight. One person's idea (like a grey piece of paper) had different resonance or dissonance depending on whose idea it neighbored.

It was like walking into a cathedral full of mosaic, where each piece of colored glass, though unique, loses itself in the vastness of the overall creation. The full array of those dry-erase walls seemed like a passage to a new kind of human interaction.

The assemblage of the parts—like colors, like mosaic tiles, like walls hosting ideas side-by side, like bodies in a room talking and listening—transcends the current known reality.

Society is in desperate need of seeing.

As Albers sought to open eyes, I write this book to advance the capacity of seeing. We are a species edging toward extinction if we do not address and change our behaviors to turn around global trends—including climate warming, gross inequality, and perpetuated violence, among others.

Maybe this kind of urgency for survival has been felt perennially throughout history, during other cycles of destruction or contraction that humankind has faced and caused (the bubonic plague, the Holocaust, ...)[10] But certainly this is a unique moment in history, with a unique necessity to address our destructive actions in order to preserve life.

With the aid of seeing, together we can more clearly choose and chart our path. Our views become shared and solvable in a very different manner than if each of us exists within our own individual sphere of understanding.

It's a time not only to see what we immediately face in the short term, but also to orient with a long view. It is a time to access the positive potential in ourselves and those around us, without apology, with determination.

It is a time, with open eyes, to see clearly and act.

Today's great challenges call us to (re)arrange our interior dimensions to more adequately meet current, outer realities.

generative scribing

10 Tobias Stone, "History Tells Us What May Happen Next with Brexit & Trump," 2016, Medium.com (https://medium.com/@tswriting/history-tells-us-what-will-happen-next-with-brexit-trump-a3fefd154714).

Working from the inside out, then, by unpacking my own experience over the past thirty or so years, I serve up generative scribing as one practice to aid with this larger shift.

This book is aimed at current and future scribes, with an aspiration to expand the possibility of the art form and the impact of our efforts.

It is for a broader audience, too, for those whose "markers" take shape as kitchen utensils, gardening rakes, community leagues, city planning, national policy-making—you name it. By replacing words like "draw" with "cook," or "wall" with "table," the meaning can translate to a variety of contexts.

This is a book for anyone who cares about how we exist together as human beings, for anyone who wants to explore their interior functioning, for anyone who seeks to approach the world anew.

about this book

This volume is not intended as an instruction manual, but rather as an approach to the practice of generative scribing, which I consider to be one discipline among many that can help us collectively orient.

In the following pages you will find numerous references to pioneers of collaborative design, dialogue, system dynamics, presencing, and related social technologies. Scribing alongside practitioners in these fields has offered me a unique opportunity to convey their findings visually, while sharing an ongoing inquiry into human potential. Most figures in the appendix, which I refer to throughout the book, result from these partnerships.

I often use "we" to refer to myself and my fellow scribes and the ideas coming from discussions we've shared. In doing so I also intentionally embrace an ecosystem mindset, choosing to write from a "future-state" of shared, heightened awareness. In other parts, the use of "I" refers to my own practice, which can tend to have a spiritual, mystic leaning.

A primary model of practice structures this collection. The model provides an overview and explains the various frameworks that have influenced my development. Each section after that addresses a primary domain within the model. And in each domain, I map some key aspects of inner cultivation that support the more visible act of drawing.

To the right is a quick overview of the book's flow:

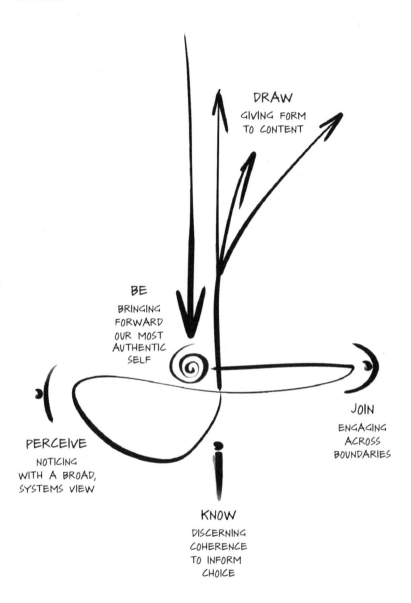

DRAW
GIVING FORM
TO CONTENT

BE
BRINGING
FORWARD
OUR MOST
AUTHENTIC
SELF

JOIN
ENGAGING
ACROSS
BOUNDARIES

PERCEIVE
NOTICING
WITH A BROAD,
SYSTEMS VIEW

KNOW
DISCERNING
COHERENCE
TO INFORM
CHOICE

When we scribe, we integrate all of these practices in fluid motion. It's not a step-by-step progression; rather it's a kind of dance sequence, an improvisational choreography, that happens during each instant of our crafting.

The book can be read in the same non-linear way. I encourage you—the participant-reader—to jump around at will, mark up the pages, and dog-ear the corners with gusto. Pass over what you don't need today. Find what resonates and dwell there.

May this slim volume greet you like the promise of a crisp spring morning: buds on branches, flocks of migrating geese overhead, drops of water falling off icicles in final melt, with longer days of light to come.

Absorb it all with ease, in right timing, with wonderment.

model of
practice

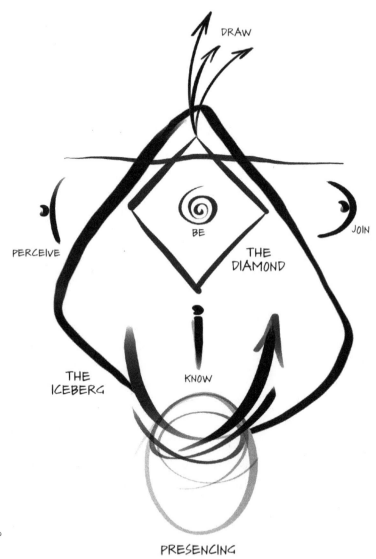

DRAW

BE

THE
DIAMOND

PERCEIVE

JOIN

THE
ICEBERG

KNOW

PRESENCING

model of practice

As we approach an action, we prepare. Just as a cake doesn't go in the oven before all the ingredients are combined, a scribe doesn't draw before processing what is being said.

It's a swift processing that stays in motion, until the very last word in a room is spoken. A scribe's preparations happen on multiple tracks, as if we are making cookies *and* muffins in rapid sequence, while simultaneously mixing and baking.

This model of practice addresses the internal coordination required to process multiple inputs and draw in real time, attending inward and outward at once.

I have developed this model through numerous attempts —over twenty years working alongside masters of human, organizational, and social dynamics—to explain scribing.

One way to explain what we do is: "We draw while people talk." And in that "while" are the active components of this framework: the domains Be, Join, Perceive, Know, and Draw. These domains are held within a "container," where trust breeds confidence, informed by the field and by source.

In this section I describe three primary influences that have helped shape these domains and that inform my model:

1. **The Diamond**, to support stance and action

2. **The Iceberg**, to enhance perspective

3. **Presencing**, to place oneself in the emerging future —related to containers, field, and source

This thinking and this model are not meant to discourage the strength of the hand and the value of the production of illustrative graphics. Indeed, that aspect of our craft is critical; it is, after all, the visual language that ultimately communicates with a participant-audience.

Rather, this thinking is meant as a foundation for scribes who want to learn and expand their practice, to better articulate aspects of what scribes do, for themselves and for others.

With this framework in mind, we can manage our own balance of domains and development.

We do this while standing in front of a wall or board, processing vast amounts of information, and between sessions as we reflect and renew.

For those of you who are not scribes, the following pages can inform any design or facilitative act. Having a difficult conversation with a partner? That requires softening, attending, and container work. Want to understand how to approach a problem differently? Frame and reframe. Exploring a new career path? Discerning and envisioning will be relevant.

For scribes and non-scribes alike, any activity that calls for thoughtful intentionality can be enriched by this guide.

the diamond

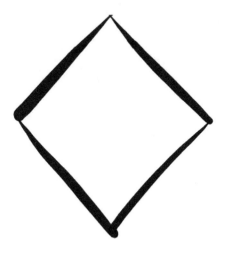

The diamond is the main structure of the model of practice (and of this book). Researchers in the fields of human and organizational development have used this shape to anchor behaviors in time, to offer a view into team and personal dynamics.[11] I've learned the following variations in different contexts and am repeatedly surprised at the depth of practice they provide, especially when layered to reinforce one another.

With all diamond frameworks, we seek BALANCE—to bring in what is missing between the parts.

---

11 Behaviors "in time" are sets of actions within a bound parameter, such as a presentation or conversation. This differs from behaviors "over time," which encompass changing conditions and outcomes. I write more about this in the chapter on time.

advocacy and inquiry

The origin of this diamond framework tracks back to
Chris Argyris and Don Schön, who presented "advocacy"
and "inquiry" as two primary axes, or stances, we occupy
in conversation. I have found that these stances underpin
everything a scribe hears: either people are advocating
—stating a view, staking a claim; or they are inquiring—
asking a question, one to which there is not an immediate
answer. An entire wall of drawing can be organized on
these positions alone.

In facilitating conversation, we want to be able to ride on either
axis. If many voices are stating their points of view, we want to
be skilled enough to invite in other perspectives. If a group is
wandering in circles, we want to be confident enough to make a
suggestion in one direction.

This applies to scribing, too. If I notice that the axes are lopsided, and I know the group seeks to have healthy conversation, I will draw up what is missing in order to prompt a balance.

If many voices are stating different points of view ("I suggest . . . " "That's not going to work . . . "), I might write them all out in equal measure. OR, I can listen closely for the few questions being raised ("I wonder if . . . ?" "Have we considered . . . ?") and emphasize those on the wall, choosing to decrease the advocacy by visually enhancing the inquiry. (See appendix Figure 2.)

Likewise, if a group is wandering in circles ("I'm not sure . . . " "This doesn't make sense . . . "), I can highlight the flow, albeit circular; OR, I can limit tracking questions and listen for the few voices that propose a solution to make sure that those are boldly noted: "Let's try . . . "

How we represent the proportion of advocacy and inquiry influences how participant-viewers understand their conversation.

People who notice a board full of single statements could wonder about the absence of questions, relatedness, and spaciousness. Likewise, people who see only open-ended phrases, connective arrows, and lots of blank space might want more definition. Again, the possibility here is in representing both advocacy *and* inquiry, while reflecting a balance of perspectives.

structural dynamics

Systems psychologist David Kantor's research in family dynamics led to a theory of structural dynamics that uncovers conversational patterns and also maps on the diamond.[12]

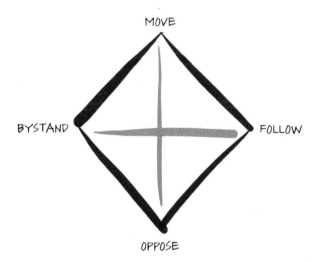

I learned about Kantor's extremely applicable Four Players in Conversation model when working closely with William Isaacs at the consulting company Dialogos in the late '90s and early 2000s.[13] My role during repeated cycles of a year-long program called "Leadership for Collective Intelligence" was primarily to document dialogic processes in words (not visually map them). This task required hours of focused attention on what people said and in what sequence, which now deeply influences how I listen.

12 David Kantor, *Reading the Room: Group Dynamics for Coaches and Leaders* (San Francisco: Jossey-Bass, 2012).

13 See also William Isaacs, *Dialogue: The Art of Thinking Together* (New York: Currency Doubleday, 1999).

generative scribing

In Kantor's model, there are four actions, or speech acts, that combine in all verbal interaction:

· **Move**, to initiate and set direction
· **Follow**, to support and complete an initiative
· **Oppose**, to challenge and correct
· **Bystand**, to witness and offer perspective

There is a big difference between "I think it's time to start planning for the next cycle." (Move) and "That sounds like a good idea!" (Follow) and "We can't start now; the team is not ready." (Oppose) and "Have we covered all our bases here?" (Bystand).

These actions are directly applicable to scribing. Referring to the above phrases, I might think to draw a timeline for Move. For Follow, a symbol of a person holding up the timeline. For Oppose, a cluster of people far from the timeline, facing another direction. For Bystand, a series of empty ovals, or some other shape to represent needed planning, between the cluster of people and the timeline.

Applied to scribing, the Four Players in Conversation model is a critical tool for noticing individual and group positions.

This tool can help us understand what is dominant and absent when one person is speaking, in any context. Some speakers are strong Movers or Opposers yet rarely question their own thinking and invite almost no audience engagement. Likewise, some speakers go to great lengths to demonstrate reflection, bringing outside learning into the room but struggling to anchor one topic. And some have a balanced blend of skills: making a case, sharing context, admitting to gaps in reasoning, seeking feedback, and standing firm in their convictions.

When scribing for a group—during a planning session or a conversation, for example—this framework also helps reveal patterns of actions and stuck dynamics. For instance, people get locked on the Advocacy axis in "point-counterpoint" (Move-Oppose-Move-Oppose) or drift in a spiral of inaction as if in a "hall of mirrors" (Move-Bystand-Bystand-Bystand) or only see their own point of view in "serial monologues" (Move-Move-Move-Move) or politely/blindly follow the leader in "courteous compliance" (Move-Follow-Follow-Follow).

Once we become aware of a particular sequence, we can listen closely for, and draw, what is missing in order to loosen or tighten the structure. In effect, as an active bystander, we notice the action that is presenting as weak, and strengthen it by how we represent the content.

If three strong movers speak in a row, each for five minutes, and then one person asks a question in just a few seconds, I would probably take key words from the first three contributions and add the whole question to the picture.

If people are meandering in meaning and keep wondering why something is happening in a certain way, and then one person suggests an action, I might synthesize the wondering into one sentence or image and then write the proposed direction up in a larger font, maybe a darker color for emphasis.

Another application of this model is detecting when a group's dynamic shifts from serial behaviors into dialogic flow. Rather than each individual speaking from their own view, each starts to move into a creative orientation, with increased inquiry into a collective, shared meaning.

This shift into flow serves, and is served by, scribing. When I sense this happening, I will start to draw an integrated rope of language over one thread, and by reflecting this coherence, it's reinforced. (See appendix Figure 3.) In this way, the art is social, since the resulting meaning of the flow of words is directly informed by multiple people.

leadership archetypes

Cliff Barry, with help from several others, founded a body of knowledge called Shadow Work®,[14] which expands the diamond to address personal development through an understanding of certain archetypes, based on the work of Carl Jung.[15]

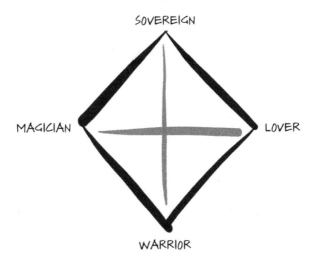

14 The term Shadow Work® is registered in the U.S. Patent and Trademark Office by Shadow Work Licensing, LLC and is used here with permission from Cliff Barry and Shadow Work Licensing (see www.shadowwork.com).

15 "Carl Jung understood archetypes as universal, archaic patterns and images that derive from the collective unconscious. They are autonomous and hidden forms which are transformed once they enter consciousness and are given particular expression by individuals and their cultures." Wikipedia, "Jungian archetypes."

I learned about the deeper application of archetypes from Barbara Cecil, Glennifer Gillespie, and Beth Jandernoa—co-founders of the Circle of Seven—in their Coming Into Your Own program for women: see www.ashlandinstitute.org.

This is an extremely subtle approach to include in scribing, where emotional gateways provide access to the various energies:

- **Sadness**, which accesses the Lover
- **Fear**, which accesses the Magician
- **Anger**, which accesses the Warrior
- **Joy**, which accesses the Sovereign

I have started each main section of this book with a chapter on one of these gateways, as sadness helps access joining, fear helps open perceiving, anger helps open knowing, and joy leads the way to drawing.

In practice, if I feel my heart swell or begin to race, if I am picking up on absence or loss, it often indicates the Lover's longing for connection somewhere in the room. I might address this by drawing in a more fluid manner, making sure to link ideas in order to increase the quality of relation.

When I sense that there is a lot of apprehension or confusion in the room—the gateway to fear—I will try to draw in a way that identifies patterns, that is clear about facts, and that presents specific options. I increase the Magician energy in the room by increasing perspective.

If there seems to be a lot of frustration in the room, I will take it as a sign that the Warrior is strongly present; therefore, I'll make sure to note decisions and concerns. People usually become angry because they care about something. Focusing on the emotion alone does a disservice to a meaningful viewpoint or a valuable contribution that someone has to offer.

And when I feel a lot of joy in the room, it's an indication of the Sovereign's energy of blessing, direction, and initiative. I will make certain to include the quality of expansion this energy brings, perhaps by writing a phrase starting with something like "Let's . . . " I'll also make an effort to draw concise next steps, a setup for action.

No one emotion or archetype is any better or worse than the others. Each one is a lens through which we see where people are coming from, and where—with our aid— they might go.

The application of the archetypes by a scribe is quite invisible work, and I often wonder if anyone in a room even knows it's happening. But I aspire to consciously balance the wall with the energy in the room, considering that one influences and reflects on the other.

All of these influences—Advocacy and Inquiry, The Four Player Model, and the Leadership Archetypes (and others not even mentioned, but of the same family)—underpin my interpretation of the diamond model.

I have tried to synthesize and simplify the terminology by using the words Join, Know, Perceive, Draw, and Be—at the center— in order to get to the essence of the domains as they apply to generative scribing.

All aspects of the diamond are needed for a complete practice. Each of us is strong in some and weak in others. Becoming aware of this imbalance and working with it, in ourselves and in service of others, is part of the learning path toward personal and professional development.

the iceberg

EVENTS		REACTIVE
PATTERNS OF BEHAVIOR		ADAPTIVE
STRUCTURES		CREATIVE
MENTAL MODELS		REFLECTIVE
VISION		GENERATIVE

The Iceberg Model, which conceptually overlays the diamond, provides a lens through which to identify leverage points for systems and the conversations that take place within them.

Edgar Schein conceived this framing of organizational culture in the early 1980s with three main layers of varying visibility: Artifacts, Espoused Values, and Assumptions. Peter Senge further developed and advanced the concept, which is now a cornerstone of organizational development around the world.[16]

The 10 percent of an iceberg that is visible above the water line represents events and action. In scribing, this is the actual drawing, the artifact, that represents what we hear.

16 Peter Senge, *The Fifth Discipline: The Art & Practice of the Learning Organization* (New York: Currency Doubleday, 1990).

The social art of scribing requires this artifact, this thing, since it comes to represent a group's co-creation and it functions to carry the group's thinking forward. If a participant-body cannot *see* what is being born of their words, then it will not be able to reflect and act on their common understanding.

Even more, the social art of scribing requires that the practitioner can recognize patterns, structures, and theories in use, as well as sense potential. This awareness helps us to understand the context behind any one word or idea, and brings both the conditions and aspiration of the system to light.

The premise of this book is that the 90 percent below the water line is as important to cultivate as what scribes draw with their ink. Especially when one considers that scribing is a social art, it is essential to address the dynamics driving the current state of interactions on, and with, the planet.

Leverage to influence social seeing and systems change increases as we move toward the bottom of the iceberg.

Diving below the water line to the 90 percent, I like to think of the layers of the iceberg in this way, from top to bottom: Patterns of Behavior, Structures, Mental Models, and (for some, though an alternative interpretation) Vision. This order correlates with action modes that are adaptive, creative, reflective, and generative.[17]

Understanding the different levels of the framework within any one situation or dynamic, we can see—and represent— an expanded picture of reality.

17 Daniel Kim, *It Begins Here: Organizational Learning Journey Toolkit* (Singapore: Cobee Publishing House, 2009).

I refer to these tiers frequently to guide my attention while listening. An initial step is to diagnose from where a person, panel, team, or whole group is speaking. What are they aiming to achieve? And how can I intentionally scribe to facilitate dialogue within their comfort zone and expand it, if that would be helpful?

I consider scribing one tier deeper than the current reality in the room. If a speaker is talking about events, or speaking factually, I become curious about the behaviors that caused those events. If a group is functioning at a behavioral level, I wonder about the structures in play.

This thought process is mostly going on in my mind and is not necessarily visible in the drawing. But my current belief is that attending in this way can actually deepen the broader conversation and bring to the surface aspects of thinking and connection that might not initially be obvious, or even known.

Applying the Iceberg Model while listening and drawing is one of the practices that can shift the scribe's stance from "visual note taking" to "graphic facilitation" to "generative scribing."

To work with an emerging future reality, we not only reflect back what is being said—the already known—but also engage in a co-discovery *with* the system in a room.

Here is a breakdown of the model, as applied to visual practice. Keep in mind that I am describing it from the top to the bottom. The drawings included in the appendix, though, follow the delivery of a presentation, which came out in another order (Structure, Patterns of Behavior, Events, Mental Models, and Vision). I have mapped this image to show how I keep this model in mind while drawing and connecting concepts.

Events are like data, actual occurrences that we see, above the metaphoric water line, like noticing a lone bird flying.

In the spoken word, I think of events as individual notes —words or phrases, single statements, ideas, comments, parts. These combine to tell stories and can be most readily represented through stand-alone pictures, such as the ovals in appendix Figure 7. This example, and the ones that follow, come from a climate simulation led by professor John Sterman, director of the MIT System Dynamics Group.[18]

Patterns of behavior convey moving parts within structures. A flock is a formation based on a need, such as the need to head south for winter. We can look for flock-like patterns in content itself and in the ways people speak. In Figure 6, Sterman was describing the increase of CO_2 emissions that leads to ocean acidification, sea-level rise, freshwater stress, and drought.

Structure shows how pieces of the picture relate to support and drive behavior. Connections across gaps become apparent, and it's the scribe's place to organize them into an order that people can perceive.

We don't look for one bird; we look for two, for three, four, forty birds and then inquire into what holds them together. Are they siblings? From different flocks? Do they face each other, or turn away? Join? Avoid? Does one bird communicate to another bird on another branch? In another tree? What are the conditions of the tree? Protected? Exposed? The answers to these questions are the components of the structure *inside* a story. Every piece of the picture offers context.

18 See C-ROADS climate policy simulator, Climate Interactive, www.climateinteractive.org.

Sterman started his simulation by naming "fossil fuel-driven economic growth" and deforestation, which—in breaking down the picture—I interpret as structures that lead to increased CO_2 emissions. (See appendix Figure 5.)

Mental Models are images we carry in our heads of how things work, to help us explain why things function as they do. For a scribe, it's challenging to make explicit the mental models of a speaker, since we are representing what we perceive, influenced by our beliefs. When someone says, "This will lead to market domination," all kinds of bells and whistles go off in my brain. My own thinking, based on my experience, colors what I hear from others. It's unavoidable.

In the iceberg drawing opening this chapter, I drew an egg and a bird to represent the mental puzzle that asks "Which comes first?" and challenges our thinking about where life begins.

Sometimes my thinking aligns with that of the presenter —such as Professor Sterman and his concern about climate change. (See appendix Figure 8.) We agree that humans buying diesel-fueled boats came before rising sea levels. Sometimes understanding the reasoning behind another's view is a challenge. No matter how many versions of "it's cyclical" I hear regarding climate, I can never seem to accept that position.

This territory is delicate; there are beliefs in the room, and there are (possibly different) beliefs in us. As scribes, we try to accurately represent what we hear and resist layering in our own thinking.

That said, with generative scribing, where we operate with awareness from an emerging sense of possibility, we can help reveal bias in order to activate reflection, and, perhaps, shift mindsets. We do this for ourselves and, as scribes, for others through our drawings. We assume that views are not fixed.

Vision is the deeper territory of aspiration, hope, calling, that which can set the tone for all else, pushing upward through the iceberg to touch the other levels. A generative scribe can sense this, and then hold the possibility in spirit (even without drawing) to join the system as its future self, and share a hope for the vision to take shape through the thinking and action of the people in the room.

I usually try to leave space on a surface for vision to come into the picture. (See appendix Figure 9.) And if it does not enter the room on the day of the session, then it wasn't meant to, and perhaps it will at another time.

It's relevant to note that the example I use in the appendix is one I have parsed out years after actually making the drawing. Originally, my only aim was to track the simulation!

Now, I realize the indispensable service this framework provides during every stage of a session—in preparation with clients, while drawing, and when digitally enhancing work for distribution—to notice, and choose, where to focus attention.

presencing

"*Presencing, the blending of* sensing *and* presence, *means to connect with the Source of the highest future possibility and to bring it into the now.*"[9]

A colleague from the Presencing Institute, Marian Goodman, has described it as "holding compassion for consciousness as it tries to find its bearings," which very much resonates with my personal experience.

generative scribing

19 C. Otto Scharmer, *Theory U: Leading from the Future as It Emerges* (San Francisco: Berrett-Koehler, 2009), p. 163. I refer many times in this book to the work of Otto Scharmer, with whom I have collaborated closely for over a decade, and whose thinking I find inextricably woven with my own.

I consider presencing to represent *being with*. It is our place at the center of the diamond and can infuse all parts of our practice. It can be experienced in a moment of time, and over time, depending on our ability to sustain a connection to our purest and most authentic Self.

The social technology of presencing is a way of being, and is foundational to a generative scribing practice.

Presencing is acting in the moment, as called for by an emerging, unfolding reality. Combining presencing with scribing leads me to pause before drawing, to expand my attention to someone's voice, the space around it, the system, the social field. In the moment before lifting a pen, I imagine the extended range of connection between people in the room and outside it, the meaning of the session in their culture, the context of their work in the context of society. I also consider our moment in time and our placement in the span of time.

Through the lens of presencing, we can represent a new possibility coming to light and chart a path from the past to the present to the future which holds that very possibility.

While presencing, I listen to my most in-tune self for guidance. I engage all of my senses to discern when to move and when to be still, when to start and when to stop. This can be by drawing or by making a comment, offering a hug, joining or leaving a group; it can be with partnership, with any kind of life decision.

Today, scribing is an individual two-dimensional art form (technology will undoubtedly shift this in the coming decades), and scribes can access presencing in themselves, individually.

01

But if the room is not aware of shifts in consciousness, scribes can only go so far with their own process; a limit in collective awareness limits the depth of the manifestation.

Likewise, the deeper the understanding a group has of presencing, the richer the container—the shared holding space—and the more qualitatively robust the drawing that results. (See appendix Figures 10 and 11.)

In graphic recording, or graphic facilitation even, the primary client need is usually to have as much literal content as possible and function with tangible knowns. But in generative scribing, it's essential to access this place of presencing, since it informs the very essence of what is trying to take shape from the *unknown*.

The times when I have stopped drawing, put my arms down, turned around to reconnect with a speaker, paused, tuned in to the moment—whether to notice rain on the roof or light bouncing on a wall at a certain angle or the cool temperature of the air—are when my internal rhythm starts to slow down, to make way for a finer sensibility to come online. My aperture of awareness opens, and more of the moment can come *through* me.

When experiencing shared presencing, there is an extreme harmony in the air—everything falling into place—and my drawing naturally mirrors that cohesion. Someone speaks a word, and I have already started to write it. I have an inclination to make a large gesture, and do, and then minutes later a speaker will add a new major topic that makes sense of my arc.

Presencing is not exercising intuition or projecting some sort of ideal state. Rather (in my interpretation) it is aligning within wholeness and, from that place, revealing the parts necessary to engage forward movement.

containers

Around the diamond, the iceberg, and presencing
—supporting these states of being and diagnostic methods—
are what I've already referred to in this book as containers:
holding spaces for places, people, and states of the heart.

*The weakness or strength of a container
determines the likelihood for detrimental
or successful conversation, for harmful
or loving relations, for destructive
or productive environments, for ill-
or well-being.*

In a way, just as ice forms from and melts back into a pond,
containers provide energetic ground for life and death,
for growth and decay. We serve as containers for others, and
they for us. The stronger a container, the stronger the trust,
the stronger the safety, the more that can be nourished,
tended, grown, realized.

Here's an example. As my grandmother Margaret Bird was aging, at a point when she could only go outside with a walker and physical assistance, we would occasionally lunch at a local diner in New York City. She would ask me things about my life, about school, about my friends, about my studies, and she would marvel at the complexity of the world in which I lived. (This was 1984, so we can only imagine what she would say about our world today!)

What I recall most poignantly is the way she paid attention, seeming to hang on every word, and the way she made me feel safe and loved—loved no matter what I said, no matter what I had to share. I never felt judged. No matter what she thought about the details of my escapades, she listened closely, looked me in the eye, and continued to pursue an understanding of my life.

She provided a container, a space where I could see myself more clearly and grow as direct result of how she was holding me.

In my work as a scribe, I try to reinforce the container for the group. When a group heats up and fractures, the container needs to strengthen, to better support what wants to come to light. I don't do this by adding a specific line or word to a page, but by enhancing my quality of listening and building the group's trust in my very being. I turn around, and see the group, feel it, open my heart to the individuals, try to put myself in their seats, find human-to-human compassion, soften, expand.

Sometimes the container in the room is so strong that the scribe might be enveloped in its power. Our ability to "show up" increases because the room is holding us, in a way, as my grandmother held me so well, years ago. In this case, I notice the strength, thank the heaven and earth for the quality of the group, and draw with pure joy.

When my grandmother, somewhat hard of hearing and surely with many of her own personal concerns, was able to show up for me so completely, I was completely able to show up for her too. I could be more vulnerable because I felt safe. She brought out the purest part of me by how gracefully she held me in her own heart.

Love, as a base note, is the ore, and order, of the container.

field

Finding a way into field . . .

"Field" can refer to a physical place, like a piece of land that holds a crop. And field can refer to an area of interest. In a social context, field also refers to a body of people and their interactions.

Field can even extend to the concept of "interbeing" —a term defined by Thich Nhat Hanh to convey the interconnectedness of all things:

"If you are a poet, you will see clearly that there is a cloud floating in this sheet of paper. Without a cloud, there will be no water; without water, the trees cannot grow; and without trees, we cannot make paper. So the cloud is in here. The existence of this page is dependent on the existence of a cloud."[20]

With the notion of field in mind, we can consider the web of relations from which, into which, and for which we draw.

20 Thich Nhat Hanh, *Being Peace* (Berkeley, CA: Parallax Press, 1987), p. 53.

My grandfather Junius Bird was an archaeologist in Central and South America from the 1930s to the 1970s, where he discovered textiles that helped identify pre-ceramic cultures. Walking through a windowed entranceway outside the front door of his home, I would pass shelves of little objects—treasures brought back from faraway places, gifts from colleagues, and curiosities found down the street. Though only about ten feet long, it was a hall of wonder, full of handmade artifacts that offered transcendence to another time and place, another culture, to some human spirit other than my own.

Because of this early seeding, that objects embody life's spirit, I have come to believe that scribed images can also contain and carry forward energy. What if, as generative scribes, we consider that each image we create holds and transfers a kind of spirituality? And what if we consider the field to be an energetic place from which we source spirit?

And what if the field is, more specifically, an energetic array of the interaction of all life—social, between people, and extending to all living matter—and it is from within that array that we draw?

As my grandfather dug up textiles from one kind of physical field to inform an understanding of human culture, generative scribes can intentionally create images that will inform current and future understanding of the human spirit.

Wassily Kandinsky defined the role of abstract art in the 20th century by writing: "The work of art mirrors itself upon the surface of our consciousness."[21] What artists create is a direct reflection of their interior condition.

21 Wassily Kandinsky, *Point and Line to Plane* (New York: Dover Publications, 1979). First translated in 1947 for the Solomon R. Guggenheim Foundation from the original publication in 1926.

I propose that this is the century in which artists consciously extend our consideration from the spirit of one to the field of many.

We can represent planes of human interaction, yes, as in a stakeholder map or an organizational chart or a Venn diagram. And we can represent individual spirit.

We can also give language to an intangible—yet perceived— quality of interaction that exists around and between seemingly disparate parts (of species, of the planet.)

As generative scribes, we can seek to represent what is beyond images that characterize inner life or the literally spoken word. Our marks are not a series of impositions on a surface; instead they represent something inherent that arises *from* a surface and *from* the field.

Fields, therefore, inform form.

One day, musing on the visual representation of fields, I started remembering previous depictions: crosshatches, flecks, washes of color. Then my mind wandered away from the language describing field back to an experience of it, an *evocation* . . .

A summer's day with family in Bearsville, New York . . . a small flagstone patio near a meadow . . . milkweed in bloom, teased by light . . . lit . . . let . . . let to be of nature . . . let to be free.

And now, with a child's memory of complete oneness with people and the earth, with care for the development of the profession of visual practice, with concern for our social relations and behaviors on a heating planet, and aware of the recursion between these various interpretations of field, I write.

source

Source. Life force. Aliveness.

Around us, in us, a wellspring of energy to tap into
at any moment.

Palpable when we feel our own heartbeat, and when we
have our head close to someone's chest and can hear theirs.

A current felt between people, living things, objects, in nature.
A vibrational, charged space. We know it when we look into
someone's eyes—when our focus on outer appearance blurs
and we meet the inner truth of that person, no matter how
well we know them.

Maybe it's in the cry of an infant at birth. Maybe it's the last gasp, the "death rattle" we hear when someone passes. It's surely in the wind, waves, flame, and rock.

Sometimes source rages and is loud and all around us, like thunder in a summer heat storm. Sometimes it's a buzzing frenzy of flies. Sometimes it's in dandelion spores floating across an empty city lot or swirling on the surface of a puddle.

Accessing source while drawing, the mind hangs, suspended, alert and patient for a specific gesture, interior stillness in the midst of outer churning.

I often pause—sometimes for a few minutes even—before drawing. I take a moment to settle, to "Be." People have asked me about this "waiting." It's partly to clear the mind, and yes, partly to sense into source.

Accessing source while drawing, what is meant to be revealed in the present moment becomes perfectly clear.

Source is a self-sustained, inextinguishable resource. We need only to be quiet, open, and breathe in to engage in its current, to infuse our own process of joining.

By attending to source, the essence of what wants to be seen makes itself known, and drawing shifts from a quick repetition of marks made *onto*, to a series of fluid marks extracted *through*. The scribe, pen, surface, words, people, room, moment all exist in harmony.

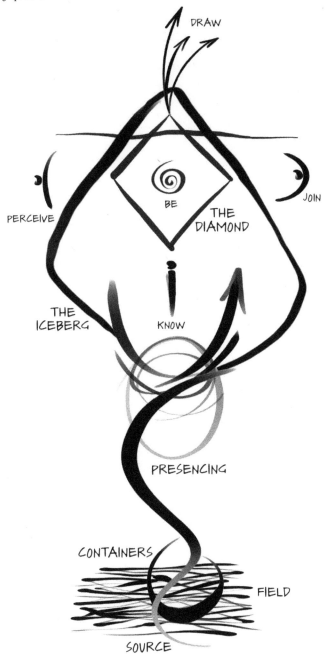

be

Everything has appearance and essence, shell and kernel, mask and truth. What does it say against the inward determination of things that we finger the shell without reaching the kernel, that we live with appearance instead of perceiving the essence, that the mask of things so blinds us that we cannot find the truth?

– Franz Marc

be

Anchored to the ground below, feet with roots;
reaching to the sky, head with limbs and leaves touching light;
extending through the heart to the wall, and the system at large.[22]

This is where my practice now begins.

The channel is strengthened between the vertical and horizontal axes. I am readying. With every in-breath I receive what wants to come through. With every out-breath my body relaxes into the moment.

Sometimes the pressure of the moment creates a false sense of ego; to perform I sometimes assume a superhero avatar, like Wonder Woman wearing armor, something that provides shielding so that I can do what needs to be done.

Behind that, though, inner confidence confirms that this moment is completely intact and natural. I am here by no coincidence. I am here to serve. What comes through is the exact gesture that needs to be revealed. No more, no less.

Being matters. If I operate from a false self, from a self that turns toward outer measure and pride, I risk making decisions based on expected outcome. Operating from a false self is like saying "I love you" to someone only in order to hear it back.

Do I draw in anticipation of applause? And if none arrives, where does that leave me? Deflated, feeling unacknowledged, inconsequential?

22 I have learned this simple guidance from Arawana Hayashi, an "acharya (senior teacher) in Shambhala–a global network of meditation centers dedicated to applying mindfulness to 'creating enlightened society.'" www.arawanahayashi.com.

When I draw from the mind and hand alone, disconnected from interior knowing, I might represent an interpreted reality and miss a window to create from reality, from the inside out.

Caring for the being means caring for the shell and kernel alike.

Physically, caring for the being includes tending to overall wellness: skeletal and muscular, of vital organs, nerves, blood flow. Metaphysically, it means tending to the inner chambers of the spirit, the part of us that holds hope, aspiration, promise; that recognizes truth, forgives, accepts, loves.

Cynicism and disbelief can cloud this spirit. To work through disbelief, I imagine the possible and act from that place, asking: "What could this look like if . . . ?"

As the armor sheds, the kernel frees, with an invitation to simply BE.

Turning inward to a place of innocence—a place perhaps guarded, protected, a place delicate and fresh—a private place, safe, elemental. That's the nugget. That's the source of energy to release.

be

can't

Almost every scribe I've talked with shares some apprehension
when facing a blank wall at the start of a session. Many of us
are introverts by nature and need to summon courage to even
be at the front of a room with an audience at our back.

As we try to follow the cadence of voices and quickly make
sense of streaming words, accents, acronyms, metaphors—
and just as quickly choose what to draw—confidence can
diminish, and questioning of oneself escalates: "Am I worthy?
Why do they want me here anyway? What on earth am I
drawing? Will anyone notice if I crawl behind this easel
and hide?!"

The thought "I can't . . ." creeps in easily and perennially.
And unless we learn how to notice this running tape in our
heads and abruptly turn it off in favor of another thought,
it's really, really easy to get psyched out and freeze.
And it's a slippery downhill slope.

Recently, to strengthen my core, I enlisted the help of a personal trainer named Carl.[23] When he would ask me to try a new exercise, I often found myself moaning "Oh, man, you have *got* to be kidding! I can't!" He would stop me in my tracks: "Once you decide you can't, you've pretty much guaranteed you won't."

"I can't" is a belief.

The "can't" belief festers in (some of) our psyches, ripe to burst forth and take the stage at the slightest challenge. It's a belief that I am, for example, not strong enough to lift a particular weight, not capable of sticking to a routine at the gym. Sometimes it's not about what I can or can't do, but about who I am. The belief in this case would be "I am lazy."

And here is where judgment comes in, residue from past experience that leads to the formation of belief. Something happened, we felt embarrassed, rejected even. Shame might have set in, reinforcing future choice and outlook.

As a young girl, I played municipal softball with great enthusiasm. Then at some point I tried out for a basketball squad and—after falling flat on my face when attempting a layup—was the only girl who did not make the team. My enthusiasm for sports quickly dwindled. And now, some thirty-five years later, I have Carl's voice helping to turn around a hardened belief that I'm inherently unskilled at sports.

Maybe "I can't" is a kind of stoplight, a temporary pause until we turn the light in our mind green. Maybe every "can't" is a gift in disguise, a twisted offering to reframe within the present moment to a mindset of "what if?"

23 My stint with Carl sadly ended when my drawing shoulder gave out and I had to end the training. But the lesson has certainly endured.

opening

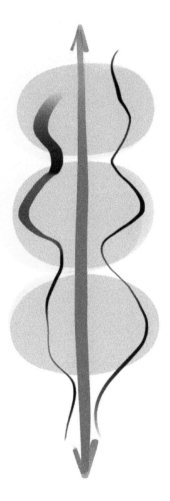

Scribes need to stay open. It's as simple as that. If we close down, we miss what is being said, get lost in our own heads, and disconnect from the flow of data and meaning that wants to be mapped. Staying open is a key skill to manage, and the challenge to do so—while listening and drawing—is constant.

There are three key capacities, defined by the Presencing work, that I actively (with mixed results) try to cultivate:

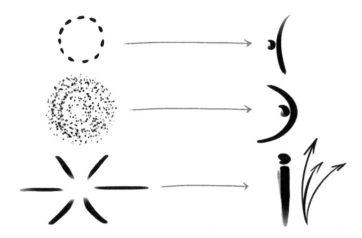

Open Mind—where with Curiosity, we Perceive

Open Heart—where with Compassion, we Join

Open Will—where with Courage, we Know and Draw

Yet quite often we encounter three voices that block the path:

1. **Judgment** restricts the Open Mind
2. **Cynicism** restricts the Open Heart
3. **Fear** restricts the Open Will

Sometimes these voices are sticky, though, and on many occasions I'd prefer a more evolved approach when I need to quickly figure out how to keep drawing. Shutting down is not an option when my back is to ten or a thousand people waiting for a picture to unfold. Shutting down is also not an option when you're a professional coach trying to offer a coachee safety, or a chef who wants to combine just the right ingredients for a tasty seasonal stew.

generative scribing

Sometimes, when I feel stuck and unable to summon any of these capacities, I turn to an exercise called "What's at Risk?"[24] In essence, it goes like this: When facing a dilemma, a coach asks: (1) "What's at risk if you do this?" And a coachee responds by listing the risks that seem possible.

Then the coach asks: (2) "What's at risk if you do not do this?" Again the coachee responds with all the perceived risks if nothing were to change.

In playing out the two sides of a stuck situation, the needed move—and the acceptable risk—becomes clear.

Sometimes I can move through stuckness and engage a more adventuresome part of myself. And sometimes, when the risk feels too high, I need to choose an action that feels more safe. And I know that either choice is completely fine.

What's important is to be honest internally about how far we can go and just keep going, as openly as possible.

For example, once I wanted to stay open-minded, in a room of people with political views opposed to my own, which seemed extremely difficult. The choice was between (1) censoring what I heard and drawing to align with my own values, thus misrepresenting the client's views, or (2) suspending my own judgment to inquire through their lens, thus opening my curiosity. Deciding that the risks of number 1 were too high, I chose number 2.

---

24 This exercise is loosely adapted from a technique I first learned from Barbara Cecil in the context of a women's leadership program called Coming Into Your Own. For more information, reference: Hal Stone and Sidra L. Stone, Embracing Our Selves (Novato: Nataraj Publishing, 1989).

02

Another example . . . I was at a wall, poised to listen with an open heart, and found myself deeply troubled by what I was hearing—sex workers sharing their powerful stories of living with structural abuse, advocating for victims' rights. What was at risk? (1) Getting swallowed by cynicism that the judiciary system could ever change, thinking my work there was futile, or (2) revealing sympathy for the victims and not accurately tracking all parts of the system in play. I chose number 2.

And another . . . I had momentarily gone numb on stage, with the pressure of being filmed and projected on a large screen in a conference hall. I had a terrifying fear that my mind would literally stop processing while someone was speaking. I had no open will, and I faced this choice: (1) draw what I did understand, even if it was very little, or (2) don't draw at all. I chose number 1.

In most cases, whenever inner noise gets in the way of tangible progress, multiple factors will inform the eventual freeing up and movement of energy. Choosing between risks is just one option. What I try to remember is this:

By staying open we become a channel for what wants to come through. We scribe to be of service to something that wants to be seen. By overcoming our inner voices we enable that service.

authenticity

By acknowledging our limits and tapping into our natural talents, we overcome our deficits and find true strength.

When first learning to scribe, I was intimidated by colleagues who could draw pictures of people, animals, buildings, and objects from memory. Some people have this innate ability. They pick up a pen and quite naturally start drawing on the wall. They listen. They draw. It seems as simple as that! But that was definitely not my experience.

After one or two years of dedicated journaling, where I wrote words alongside sketches, I realized that my style— my true voice—was going to have to be something new, to me and to others. It would be some mix of what I knew my hand *could* shape, and a method of processing that was unique to my brain. (See appendix Figure 12.)

What resulted was an organic, nature-based approach that represented how I saw and made sense of the world.[25] I stumbled quite a lot in private and in public while figuring this out. And my strength—bringing coherence to the surface—only became clear after many years of awkward and aching experimentation.

And this leads to the point of authenticity. When learning to scribe, I emulated others. As part of a team facilitating collaborative workshops, I would literally "wall-copy" to document the work, which is an excellent introductory

25 The approach I developed was largely shaped by Bryan Coffman, of the MG Taylor network, who drew kidney-shaped models that created context for complex interactions. He showed me that natural form can hold all thinking.

way of building the scribing skill.[26] But it required personal and professional diligence to uncover our own unique gifts and give them shape.

We grow when we follow our curiosity—whether by working with leading thinkers, visiting museums, or exposing ourselves to other disciplines and art forms. Our view of things shifts with each new vantage point, like walking a route that we normally drive, or flying above a field of grain we are used to seeing as cereal in a bowl.

We settle into our more authentic self when we start to listen to our internal voice, the one that says: *"This is true. Yes."* To the impulse in the gut: *"Okay, go with it."* +To the heat rising through the veins: *"This matters."*

As we hear these messages and listen to them—as we would take advice from a mentor or a coach—we inhabit our truest self, the one that has been waiting years for us to grow up, to show up.

We learn by copying. We advance through integration. We master by tapping into our own source.

26 Wall-copying was a method we used in the ASE, before digital cameras, to record drawings on whiteboards. Using a clipboard and a set of pens that exactly matched the colors of the dry-erase markers, each "knowledge worker" would copy the handwriting and images from a wall onto an 8.5 x 11" sheet of paper. We did dozens of these in one three-day DesignShop™, hundreds in a few months.

cultivation

Scribes are reflective aids. Information filters through us on its way to a participant-audience. Because it's an active process, the filter needs regular tending to work effectively.

If we do not take care of the inner landscape, our awareness, we risk blind behavior—drawing beautifully, but missing how we are part of an unfolding reality.

Without paying close attention, I risk skating over the surface of deeper potential. I won't be able to recognize the fineness of something new coming to light—like a very quiet voice in a room saying the one thing no one wanted to say, the one thing that might reroute the path and tone of a conversation.

A potter's clay is tangible, as the scribe's drawing is visual. But the scribe's medium is cultivating social awareness, which requires a different approach to shaping.

To grow, I have tried to locate my best self—the self that accepts, that chooses possibility over apprehension and frustration, the self that welcomes the new and even carves a path for it. With this orientation, I imagine serving as a microcosm of reorientation for every part of a system that my drawings might touch.

My first experience of this occurred sometime in 2006, when working with the Ashland Institute on a long-term project for the Girl Scouts of Arizona. My role was mostly to document and archive the output from multiple discussions among council staff, elders, and volunteers. My explicit purpose was to translate the group's learning from verbal reflection into tangible form, to be shared with other councils and the national system.

During one session near Sedona, Arizona—in a cabin with fifteen other women nestled amongst forest and red rock and a nearby creek—I remember one pivotal conversation. Each person had gone into nature for an hour and a half to find her place in silence, to listen to her heart and "let come" a deeper wisdom. After they returned to the cabin I scribed while each woman shared her insights.

The drawing I produced was full of their revelations:
"This is a hologram of the whole." "Serve as a beacon; I am the
organization." "Guide the deliberate and allow for emergence."
And I recall the shift in me with each verbal sharing; some
kind of larger participatory transition was also under way.
I was standing at a wall in this small room, the women
were in a circle, charts covered the walls. Each contribution
(verbal, drawn, gestured, even pregnant pauses) extended and
deepened the others. Each voice spoke for the whole.

I was not just a scribe on the periphery of the gathering, but
belonged in this constellation that held a promise for more
than 1.5 million girls. I was drawing for my colleagues and the
clients in the room; and I was drawing to facilitate a cultural
turning, the scope of which was beyond what any of us could
have logically considered.

Scribes contribute to activating social fields by showing up from the inside out.

As we cultivate our practice over time, health matters.
Mental clarity matters. The state of the heart matters.
If any of these aspects weaken or become stale, how
can I stay ready, for myself, for others?

As my hand has matured and drawn increasingly refined lines,
so has my inner attunement grown to guide my decisions.
Learning to say no to certain work opportunities, for example,
takes determination to clarify the yeses. Neither response
comes lightly, and both require a clarity of mind I still
seek to develop.

I can let my mind slip into habit and draw a picture from
memory. That might help me on a day when I'm sleepy or jet
lagged. But over the long term my growth stagnates if I don't
absorb new information and experiment.

zone

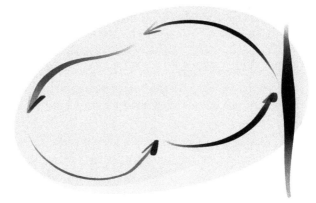

When I scribe, on the best of days I connect with a zone. I call this a reciprocal zone, because it's not only about how I relate to threads of understanding; it is also about the inescapable web of gesture and impact in which I find myself.

My mind, heart, hand, the drawing surface, the markers, the people behind me and around me, the bounds of the room, the building, all of the people supporting what is happening in the room, people who have come before and fueled the current thinking, people who will carry forward today's ideas, the system(s) beyond the walls that the group is part of . . . all are threads in this web.

Our points of connection manifest a series of reinforcing loops, where the insight of one touches the insight of another, and the stuckness of one person can influence the stuckness of another. While drawing, on the best of days, I know and can sense this activation.

The quality of being I bring to any given moment, my energy, ripples out to reinforce the surround. This is not to say that

generative scribing

scribes are magicians who weave some sort of spell—
absolutely not! Everyone has access to the energy field of
which I write. But, as artists, we do work with intangibles
in a conscious, often invisible, way.

I am a bystander, and then an active participant with the
people in the room and the system. My role is to create a
path for something else to come into existence and light.

We connect to an inner place of wonder,
and thus we are open to recognizing the
spirit of wonder in the world around us.

On clear days my presence, my quality of being, allows me to
show up for a group during any phase in their process, to hold
a space of possibility for what might develop. Part of locating
presence has to do with suspending thoughts and habits of
judgment, letting go of the past and also of the projections of
the future, so we can be completely in the moment and join a
group where they are, in order to co-create from that place.

To explore presence is to learn a language that is not literal,
but is internal and is very much embodied, if initially faint.
We might ask ourselves: What are the barriers, between fear
and fluency? How do we feel different when we are at ease?
When we are in a position to express, what language do we use?

This piece of the practice is not about
aesthetics. This is the intangible dimension,
where we are in touch with ourselves at the
truest level and in a position to meet the
truth in the room through what we draw.

It is breathtaking to sense the flow, the presence of many. To
work in that place, to give form to the unexpressed—that is the
magic of the reciprocal zone that our presence merely meets.

join

*The goal of life
is to make your heartbeat
match the beat of the universe,
to match your nature with Nature.*

– Joseph Campbell

join

To join is to meet ourselves where we are, to meet others where they are, and together meet the world where it is.

Alone, I can join more deeply with myself, with my own heartbeat. Sometimes silence and warm tea provide all the company I need to settle into my core rhythm.

When joining with others—receiving their edge or their tenderness, their apprehension, their exuberance—I care about their state of being, their wellness, their suffering.

When joining strangers at a café or conference attendees in a foreign country, I notice our similarities, our differences, and that we all walk on the same ground.

Boundaries dissolve when we activate our deeper humanity.

When talking with a small child, I bend down so we are at eye level with each other. Greeting a client or colleague, I shake hands or offer an embrace. Before petting a dog for the first time, I extend my hand to its nose so that it may know my scent. Walking at ocean's edge, I curve with the waves rolling in out.

Perhaps in body, we live each day and die alone. But in heart, in spirit, we start and end each moment infinitely entwined.

With this orientation we are not separate.
Your concerns are my concerns.

Every seam, two neighboring parts.
Every line of division, an opportunity for a join.

sadness

"Horas non numero nisi serenas."
(I count only the happy hours.)

—Quote from the wrapping of a Baci chocolate
(a Latin phrase also likely inscribed on a sundial somewhere)

October 27, 1987, Santa Maria Formosa, Venice, Italy. I was
21 years old, sketching during a weekend trip with friends.
We were fortunate to be studying abroad, and the quotation
above crystallized a time in my life of great expansion,
comradery, learning at every corner—a time when
happiness was all around me and in me.

And yet . . . as I sat and drew an empty piazza at the side of
a Renaissance church with a smooth, straw-colored plaster
exterior and deep-set, wooden-shuttered windows, watching
pigeons strut around a covered water well—more taken with
my oil pastels and solitude than with joining anyone or any
spirit inside the building—I also wrote this:

"But happiness cannot come without sadness; the two equal all
the hours. I count all the hours. But the happy ones are made that
much more special by those that are sad. Contrast."

This was my learning from Venice, a city of sweeping,
open public spaces against canals of private, off-limits
homes. Throngs of tourists shopping for the latest fashion
contrasted with cathedral floors warped from centuries of
flooding. Celebrities in gondolas with paparazzi in tow, lone
art students in squares.

I've written much about sadness in journals over the years, as it's a close friend who knocks often. But I need look no further to be able to say this now . . .

Sadness connects us to the nuance of life, grey pause to the color of activity.

Without knowing grey, we might overlook subtle indicators of variety. Grey is akin to the quiet voice in a room that counters assertion, the trailing end to a sentence that provides a moment of digestion, the in-breath before a sigh or an exhale. When scribing, I might not draw these subtle verbal tones, but they certainly influence the way I attune to a broader range.

As light dims, as every fall reabsorbs the leaves into the ground, as nature collapses inward to retreat through winter, so spring follows. Bulbs, once dormant, burst forth. The chartreuse of spring and the gold of summer return. Harmony.

As in nature, emotions cycle. Sadness passes. Joy returns.

Sadness asks us to notice the cracks, the subtleties, to slow down, to find a wider range of inclusion, to consider the shady valley and thus see more clearly the sun-kissed mountain.

soften

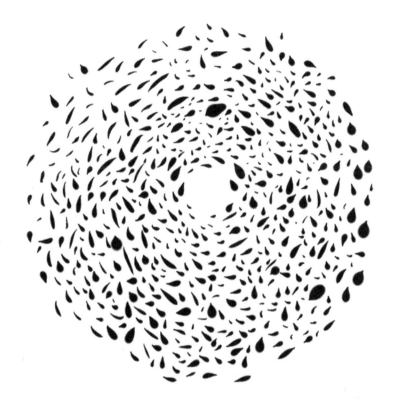

We soften to be of service, when showing up, when waiting, while preparing to join, before making any mark.

Like an apple ripe for picking, we, too, require preparation and maturation to be in season, of service. There is a prime condition required for facilitative work. Too hard: unyielding, sectioned off. Too soft: malleable, en route to collapse.

But unlike nature ripening in its time, we must learn to soften appropriately, and intentionally, in any given moment. Being poised to receive takes inner work that is not always in sync with outer demands. A technology run-through with strobing lights, for example, can easily interrupt this gentler internal rhythm.

To respond to the demands of others and of preparation is necessary, yes. But the required "on" stance can sometimes produce rigidity. If overdone, it can cause us to split off, reinforcing a dualistic mentality: me | technician . . . me | content . . . me | ME . . . my "show up and do good, concerned with impression and reward" self | my true SELF, the one with the most insight to offer a given situation.

With barriers in place we do protect ourselves from possible negative scenarios, such as misunderstandings, complaints, scope creep. This is how we keep projected disappointment in check. But by doing so we also risk living with a closed-off sensibility.

There is a correlation between what we let in and the fineness of our perception, which then informs our choice and output.

As we "steel up" we stand guarded, sectioned off. As we soften, we open, we are touched. Touched, we feel. Additional senses come online. Defenses relax. Attunement strengthens. Range expands. Listening increases. Insight opens.

We meet an intuitive knowing—beyond literal understanding of words and concepts. Because we are relaxed, we receive and join as porous beings—not merely sponges, only absorbing, but as enhanced conduits for flow-through of meaning.

Gentle reminders to myself, in picking up a marker:

Soften assumptions, beliefs, judgments. Name them.
Own them. Check them at the door. Step in front of the
wall. Pick up a marker. Slightly lower your arm, as a step
toward lowering your guard.

Soften to see another's point of view. Soften to let yourself
be moved (even to tears).

Soften to hear the hum of the room, to take in and let out
your breath.

Soften to notice the beat of your heart, to notice another's.

Soften to feel joy, grief, anger, confusion. Soften to hear and
acknowledge these emotions, then facilitate transformation
by inquiring inside and beyond them.

Soften to be strong. Trust that in softening we will not dissolve
or be hurt; rather we will expand to meet what comes our way
and further o p e n.

attend

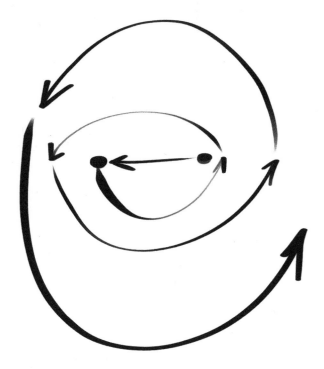

Increase the sphere of attention. Expand the outer skin of the whole. Tune in. Awaken.

In the practice of scribing, I attend to many tiers: to my own being, to a group in the room, to an organization the group represents, to the culture of that organization, to the society within which the culture forms, to the planet . . . and depending on how far out we want to go—to the Universe.

I attend to these realms individually, and often simultaneously, as is necessary, as is possible.

In any given moment at a wall, we have multiple demands on our concentration.

I hear a word, or the noise of a clicking Bic pen, or my growling stomach, or my aching feet.

And/or I hear a drowning monologue swarming in the air and my mind fills with irritation.

And/or I move outside my own bubble to more closely hear the speaker, speaking softly, voice slightly quivering. I wonder about the relationship between the speaker and the audience. I sense hesitancy.

What is going on? What wants to happen here?
Where do I attend?

I notice the range of these demands on my focus, yet attend to the specific piece that seems to need the spotlight, needs to be known, the sprout seeking sun.

By directing in this way, and drawing from this place, the clicking of the Bic pen goes away, the gurgling in my stomach subsides, the quivering voice is a sign of growth, the monologue becomes a prologue—not a series of independent thoughts to list and characterize, but a contextual thread of meaning that underpins a broader message.

Because I have shifted my direction from distraction to actual message, what I draw—and what I now hear—will naturally follow that path.

The range of attention corresponds to that which is taken in, received, and then that which is turned outward, revealed, through the hand.

generative scribing

It's an expanding relation, between receiving and revealing, and often they enhance each other. The more open I am, the more I notice. The more I notice, the more I reveal. The more revealed, the more seen. The collective attention expands, as form facilitates growth.

Dowsing rods divine water sources. In the same way, our markers lead us into the present moment. And, from that place, we draw.

listen

I have written this book in as non-linear a fashion as I expect some of you to be reading it, moving from chapter to chapter as inspired. It is the same way I approach drawing on a wall.

It's the same way I listen, through all the senses—impressionistically at first, like attending to the reflective surface of a pond, until I notice a tadpole below the water line and then a fish below that, and then glistening rocks under the fish. When drawing, I have a sense of an overall topic (water), then an organizing structure (pond). The connective tissue (the rocks) comes after the individual pieces (the tadpoles, the fish) have taken shape.

When listening, we attend to the parts, the interdependencies, and the meaning —all at once.

When listening in order to scribe in a generative way, the image that takes shape is at first vague, like a face we might see across the street, where features have order but lack definition. As the face comes into view, the shape of each eye is clearly almond. The chin, raised slightly. The mouth, curved upward at the corner, in a smile.

My engagement with the face, the person—like my engagement with the spoken word of a group—becomes clear as it nears. When across the street, or in the first ten minutes of an hour-long talk, I settle into my place on the ground and into myself to collect inputs and make sense, find meaning.

The meaning, though, does not come only after the parts, the interaction, the story. It comes alongside. Listening involves a parallel capability to notice each of these elements as they come online, as they become clear.

Listening is a through line to any generative practice.

This chapter falls almost exactly in the middle of the book, and yet I'm writing it last, perhaps because I've had to listen to what the book itself wants to say. How can I write about listening without having first reflected on the ways I listen?!

I searched these pages for what I write elsewhere in the book about listening. Here are a few excerpts:

I listen. I draw. You see. You speak. I listen I draw you see you speak. You see I listen you speak I draw. You speak I draw we see we listen. That's how it feels. It's fluid. (Introduction)

Once we become aware of a particular sequence, we can listen closely for, and draw, what is missing in order to loosen or tighten the structure. (Diamond)

I refer to these tiers frequently to guide my attention while listening. (Iceberg) (See appendix Figure 13.)

While presencing, I listen to my most in-tune self for guidance. (Presencing)

When a group heats up and fractures, the container needs to strengthen, to better support what wants to come to light. I don't do this by adding a specific line or word to a page, but by enhancing my quality of listening and building the group's trust in my very being. (Containers)

Staying open is a key skill to manage, and the challenge to do so—while listening and drawing—is constant. (Opening)

We settle into our more authentic self when we start to listen to our internal voice, the one that says: *"This is true. Yes."* (Authenticity)

As we "steel up" we stand guarded, sectioned off. As we soften, we open, we are touched. Touched, we feel. Additional senses come online. Defenses relax. Attunement strengthens. Range expands. Listening increases. Insight opens. (Soften)

So I look up the looming, unavoidable beast that is necessary to include in the picture. If I do not include it, it will be obvious that I've bypassed the mention of the topic, or it might suggest a lack of listening or understanding. (Laugh)

In order to clearly represent what people are saying, I need to . . . listen carefully to detect their data . . . (Suspend)

Whether conceptual framing comes easily to you or not, consider it a quick way to structure a board and orient listening. (Frame)

At the wall, what wants to be drawn? Before making a mark, envision the mark. If you can't imagine it, don't draw it. First, deepen your listening. (Trust)

Part of choosing what to draw is subjective, based on our listening skills; part is objective, based on our ability to order and sift data; and part is generative, based on how we connect with source. (Discernment)

Different "levels" of listening can help us participate in a shift of awareness and possibility. (Levels of Scribing)

We listen to empathize and to represent. (Generative Scribing)

laugh

"One minute she's so happy
Then she's crying on someone's knee
Saying laughing and crying
You know it's the same release." [27]

How many times have these lines from Joni Mitchell saved
me in a sweat-inducing performance crunch? Countless.
When drawing is difficult—especially when needing to draw
"things" like machine parts or any object, really—I mildly panic
and want to melt into the floor. Joni reminds me of our choice
to collapse or to shake it off.

"Argggghh! That damn elephant!" I moan, even after drawing
one on many occasions and observing shortcuts used by other
scribes. But each time I still shake my head and look it up
online. And, in these moments, I realize it's time for a laugh.

Animals are the hardest for me because they are alive, and it
seems that a two-dimensional drawing never, ever captures
the aliveness of the real thing.

Goat? *Okay.* Camel? Ox? Cat? Rat? Each mention of a creature
inhabits me like a gulp of sour milk. (I am even cringing now as
I write.) "Elephant in the room . . ." *Well, everyone's heard that.*
Everyone knows what that means. No need to draw it, right?

So I search for the looming, unavoidable beast that is necessary
to include in the picture. If I do not include it, it will be obvious
that I've bypassed the mention of the topic, or it might suggest
a lack of listening or understanding.

27 Joni Mitchell, "People's Parties," from the album *Court and Spark*
    (Asylum Records, 1974).

I therefore look up the the goat, the camel, the ox, the cat, the rat, the elephant, and make my best attempt. And then, inevitably, I laugh.

The drawing is never clear, and always requires annotation. I snap a quick picture and text my friend and colleague Sita Magnuson who, each and every time, has always laughed with me. And in the sharing, the anxiety passes.

I know, I know. All those icon books, all those zoos, all my spare evenings—plenty of opportunity to practice. Once, even, after leading a workshop, the participants gave me a lovely book in which each had drawn an elephant on the first page after hearing this story. It warmed my heart, but ultimately did not eliminate my problem.

This drawing deficit of mine does provide an opportunity, though, to stay lighthearted, to relieve some of the seriousness that hovers around important work, to ease the self-imposed pressure of unattainable yet desired clarity, to connect with a friend while alone at a wall, to ease up.

In having fun, the heart lifts.

And through laughter I remain inside and outside myself at once, seeking to appreciate, simply, what IS.

ripples

Ripples result when leaving "me-them" polarization at the door and choosing instead an interwoven path: WE ARE ONE.

This can be a conscious, enlightened, spiritual choice.
It's also simply a matter of relaxing into the fact that through every gesture, every word, every silence even —we exist in a cascading ripple of touch.

Through doing, like carrying a bag of groceries for a stranger, we touch.

Through feeling, like noticing heart heaviness with the absence of a loved one, we are touched.

Through thinking, when my ideas linger in your mind and your ideas in mine, guiding further thinking, we touch.

To deny the impact of these ripples is to deny that we have any vibration, any aliveness. Because we breathe and our hearts pulse, we are ALIVE. We emit. We receive. We magnetize.

***Crossing invented division, through
outward and inward motion, one.***

perceive

There are no separate systems.
The world is a continuum.
Where to draw a boundary around a system
depends on the purpose of the discussion
—the questions we want to ask.

–Donella Meadows

perceive

What we see informs how we orient ourselves to draw,
to take action.

By seeing, I don't mean only the optical result of looking.
What I notice through my eyes, when staring at branches
reflected in a pond, reaches my brain and causes a sensory
response of pleasure, and might lead to noticing the relation
between light, water, and leaves.

To me, seeing is more about how we perceive our way into the
thinking, the structures, and the behaviors of systems in order
to reveal patterns and dynamics, to find leverage points, and to
shift outcomes. To see is to comprehend.

*"Perception is not just the passive recording of sensory stimuli,
but rather an active mental reconstruction of the real world that
surrounds us."*[28]

We see—we perceive—to diagnose, to comprehend, to map.

I gaze into a pond and wonder at the beauty of the reflections.
Is it only size and weight that allows a stick to float and causes
a log to sink? Do fingerlings chasing food interact with each
piece of dismembered tree differently? Which piece of tree is
absorbed sooner back into the pond floor?

Words = fingerlings. Directional lines = wood. Color = light.
Surface washes = water, land, air. Texture = leaves.

28 Rainer Rosenzweig, "Perceiving Is More Than Seeing," In the World
of the Senses, *FOCUS* (Tübingen: Max Planck Research, April 2001),
http://www.kyb.tuebingen.mpg.de/fileadmin/user_upload/files/
publications/pdfs/pdf3050.pdf.

How do I translate what I see, what I perceive, into something that makes sense to others? And not only something that makes sense, but also something that leads to insight?

What if I do not define the boundary of the pond, the edge of the conversation? What does that imply?

What if I am lost in the cadence of the speakers' voices, the beauty, and don't notice what they are saying?

What does my picture suggest if I only include fingerlings and wood—only words and direction—without offering light?

What if I include one hundred words and a small line that points to another hundred words, instead of choosing twenty-five words adjoining a medium-thick vertical line, or instead of highlighting only ten words with a thick vertical line that separates them from another ten words nearby?

These subtle distinctions matter when I'm trying to convey what I perceive. Each drawing conveys its own meaning. Connection versus dependence versus separation.

What if I get lost in my "what ifs," get tripped up in interpretation, and step back so far from the picture that there is no longer a pond with a perimeter, only a speck of deep blue in the middle of a forest?

The point is to pay attention. To notice. To stay alert. To inquire.

fear

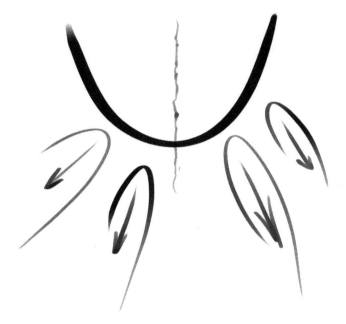

As sadness leads to joining, fear leads to perceiving.

Years ago, a friend sent me this loose quotation from Ernst Cassirer:

"The depth of human experience . . . depends on the fact that we are able to vary our modes of seeing, that we can alternate our views of reality. Art gives us a richer, more vivid and colorful image of reality, and a more profound insight into its formal structure. It is characteristic of the nature of man that he is not limited to one specific approach to reality but can choose his point of view." [29]

29 Ernst Cassirer, *An Essay on Man: An Introduction to a Philosophy of Human Culture* (New Haven, CT: Yale University Press, 1944).

I had copied the quotation onto a postcard of Paul Klee's "Farbtafel (auf majorem Grau)" / "Color Table (on Major Gray)," 1930. That the postcard seems colorful—a range of rust, slate grey, bark, wet New England earth, night sky, fog—is testament to Klee's genius. Through his experiments with perception, he could stretch the subtlety of a limited palette to its maximum nuance.

The postcard tumbled out of John Berger's book *Ways of Seeing*, which first swept me off my feet around 1987. From the book's cover:

"Seeing comes before words. The child looks and recognizes before it can speak . . . It is seeing which establishes our place in the surrounding world."

The book found me again one morning while I was trying to familiarize myself with Jungian archetypes, specifically an interpretation of Fear as a gateway to Magician energy. I was seeking guidance, having gone to bed the night before anticipating with great fear an upcoming session in which over 10,000 people would be watching me scribe, remotely, from all over the world.[30] Rationally, I knew I was ready, that everything would be okay, and that there were many people supporting my effort.

The fear was palpable, though, and to dismiss it would have negated a huge amount of energy that also resides in fear's quivering, distasteful shell. To relate to that fear, and not call it unfounded or irrational or irrelevant even, was necessary to engage it and turn it to constructive use.

generative scribing

---

30 The session was live-streamed as part of a MOOC (massive open online course) called "u.lab: Transforming Business, Society, and Self," initially delivered through MITx in 2014.

I also went to bed that night wondering about the correlation between fear and potential. Is the scope of fear proportional to the scope of possibility in my hands, in our hands?

"When two colors meet they form an edge whose enormous aesthetic potential can be realized only if the edge is treated as the occasion for drawing . . . To one side we will have solidity, hence mass; to the other, air and light."[31]

Perhaps fear is the awkward edge between the past (what is known) and future possibility (what is sensed)?

But how can I honor the whole that wants to emerge when I cannot see it? Perhaps to see it, it is necessary to orient with another point of view.

It is only by relating to the fear, and using it as fuel, that the hand will open, extend, draw.

During that hour-long session, I interpreted my fear as an indicator of some change necessary in me—"me," simply representing a small sampling of a larger change called for in the work of the global community tuning into the broadcast.

And, in order to create, I could not lie dormant. I had to get up. I needed to show up. I needed to shift my relationship to the fear. To do this, it was necessary to embrace the fear—as I wrote of embracing sadness—and somehow receive it as a gift.

31 Richard Hennessy, "The Man Who Forgot How to Paint,"
    Art in America (Summer 1984).

04

Once I remembered this, I started considering more views, more options. My efforts that day were just one dot in a sea of dots that many people were activating together. My fear was infinitely smaller than the texture formed by the possibility we were unleashing as a social body.

Fear is a key to perception, on the path to choice.

Through fear, we face uncertainty. Moving through uncertainty, we experiment. With experimentation, we experience and can perceive. Through perception, we orient. With orientation, we choose. And through choosing, we direct ourselves to act.

suspend

How often do we find ourselves criticizing what we hear someone say or judging someone's actions? I do this, way more than I care to admit. Almost every time I hear the phrase "It's not possible . . ." something inside me winces and cries: "Why is your thinking so limited?!"

Yet my closed mindset serves no one—not those in the room, not me, not the person making the statement, not whatever action is being contemplated—whether it's meeting an annual financial goal, trying to sing on key, or landing on Mars. I have punctuated a "not" with an accusation, constructing a quick double-negative, narrowing probability.

As a generative scribe, with a desire to expand rather than contract opportunity, I must continually reposition my inner landscape to suspend judgment. This requires checking in on a number of fronts: my mental models, the beliefs of the people in a room, the culture of an organization, and even the philosophies of the sector or region represented.

It is far too easy to get tripped up by my own thinking or state of being and inadvertently close my mind to what is actually going on. Sometimes, when scribing, I get overly concerned about the legibility of my handwriting and spelling. Perfectionism settles in, and I lose track of the actual sequence of spoken words. Other times I disagree with what someone is saying, and I face personal resistance to including their thoughts in the picture.

Once, at a very high-level session on global finance (where I needed a badge with a special hologram to enter the room) my nerves were ablaze facing the level of power that was present.

I went in with an assumption that there were diplomatic factors in play that would prevent qualitative conversation from taking place, and that what happened in the room would not really influence any decisions. But really, how was I to know?! (And that was not the case.)

Check the data, keep an open mind, and get out of our own way.

One fundamental framework I use to suspend judgment is the Ladder of Inference, which describes the scale of thinking between experience-based data and belief-based action.[32] Though all of the ladder's steps exist in the "now," the top of the ladder tends to waver more abstractly in memory, and the bottom lands more solidly in the present moment.

Here is an overview of the steps on the ladder:

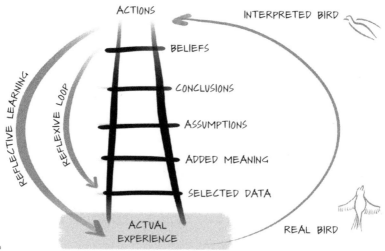

32 Peter Senge, Art Kleiner, Charlotte Roberts, Richard Ross, and Bryan Smith, *The Fifth Discipline Fieldbook: Strategies and Tools for Building a Learning Organization* (New York: Currency Doubleday, 1994), Chapter 35.

generative scribing

Beliefs: Things we consider to be true and absolute. *For someone to recognize a bird I draw, I need to represent it in flight.*

Conclusions: Decisions based on reasoning. *Birds are most recognizable in flight.*

Assumptions: Things that are accepted as true or as certain to happen. *Cardinals, and all birds, must fly around a lot.*

Added Meaning: What is interpreted or inferred from a word, text, concept, or action. *In order to find enough food every day, cardinals must fly between many backyards.*

Selected Data: Chosen facts and statistics collected for reference. *Cardinals eat off flat surfaces and come and go freely.*

Actual Experience: Practical contact with facts or events or occurrences. *Sometimes my brother and I watch cardinals feeding in his backyard.*

Reflexive Loop: The beliefs we hold on to influence our selection of future data and actions. *I draw birds in flight and watch birds coming and going, but I don't draw or watch birds on branches or the ground.*

Reflective Learning: Looking more closely to increase our understanding. *I have great difficulty drawing animals, but if I closely observe real birds in a variety of settings and take note of their range of forms, my drawing will improve.*

And here is a purely behavioral example—from life, not from scribing—starting with experience, then jumping around between the levels, as it happens:

I call my mom and ask how she's doing (based on experience). "Fine," she answers (data).

But I think to myself, "*Her voice is low and her words are slow* (data). *She does not SOUND fine*" (added meaning). "*Uh-oh. This is going to be one of THOSE kinds of uncomfortable conversations, loaded with innuendo*" (assumption).

See how fast I made that leap?!

Then I ask, "Is something going on?" I'm trying to inquire, to scale back to her actual experience. "No, I'm getting ready to go to the dentist. The plumber is coming at noon, then I'm meeting my book group" (lots of data).

But in my body, in my heart, I am hearing something else behind the words, in her tone, and still can't help thinking there is something more going on (conclusion).

I am substituting my invented reality, which in my head sounds like "*Fine does not mean fine*" (belief), for her "Fine" (data). And I'm certain that my interpretation is correct.

I think, "*My mother is hiding something. Maybe she is trying to protect me, or not bother me. And clearly she does not want to talk about it now! This will not be a substantive conversation. I might as well get off the phone.*"

Again, see how quickly I scaled back up? And in doing so I got lost in my own story about the call, became reflexive, stopped listening to my mom, and prematurely ended the call.

My belief reinforced my experience, which will likely influence how I listen and what I experience and hear in the future, leading to another trip up the ladder on a future call.

But back to how this applies to scribing . . .

In order to clearly represent what people are saying, I need to be aware of what I hear and what I choose to represent. Is someone making a conclusion? If so, I can listen for their assumptions, added meaning, and data. If those are hard to detect, then I can choose to include their conclusion, or not.

When I hear the word "future" do I assume the whole group is forward focused? Maybe some of them are hesitant or concerned, and I have stopped listening for those other voices.

To get the data to the surface requires "scaling down the ladder." As scribes, we must always return to actual words, no matter our triggers or goals for the outcomes of a session.

If something is not clear, pause. Slow down.

Check the reasoning. Turn away from the board and mentally move closer to the words, to the person speaking, to the data. Put yourself in their shoes. Inhabit another vantage point. Resist the urge to draw until you return to the ground.

This kind of real-time inquiry risks getting in the way of our needed fluid state; checking the accuracy of what we think we hear can break the momentum of attending to the next words, and the next after those. But one spot-on interpretation against a hundred misrepresented ideas is invaluable.

A scribed picture is only worth a thousand words if it represents an array of actual references.

frame

To frame is to convey boundaries—limits, openings, options. Frames help compartmentalize and also define areas that we can then bridge through relation. The framing of the physical and the framing of our thinking parallel each other. Both are needed in visual practice; I organize information in my mind *while* organizing words and shapes on a page.

One understanding of a frame is physical.

Frames can be the protective edges of a two-dimensional form, such as the frame around a window or around eyeglasses. Drawn frames can look like boxes or circles. The outer edge of the paper also represents a frame, as do the four walls of a conference room that contains a display of completed work.

We frame content to give it contextual coherence. We cluster similar ideas and surround the grouping with a closed line. But framing isn't only about boxing things in or fitting things together.

Framing is ultimately about setting up conditions for choice.

With the proportions and proximity of what we include and exclude, we provide a limit that informs the participant-viewer what is in, what is out. With that information, people can make decisions about how to place themselves relative to what the picture conveys. They join a team, or they don't. They expand a new product, or they contract operations.

Another understanding of framing is conceptual, relating to the lenses we use to organize what we hear and intuit.

I often bring in models as scaffolds for my thinking. Sometimes this happens in pre-session planning with a client; at other times it happens early and quickly at a wall, almost in the first minute. I recall the client's intent and desired outcome, which could be geared to action or reflection, and go through my memory bank for a loose structure, a sort of spine. And then I hold this structure as a backbone for how I listen.

One fail-proof framework is Robert Fritz's Creative Tension model.[33] It is frequently drawn with Current Reality on the bottom, Vision on top, and the middle section representing the creative—or structural—tension between the other two.

33 See the chapter "Choice" for an image
and for more information about this model.

I might be in a session where there is very clear aspiration and all that's needed is some grounding to establish a starting point for action.

Or, I might be listening to a conversation on strategy and notice words that indicate a conservative approach, a preference for existing conditions. People might be saying "Why fix something that isn't broken?" or "I don't know . . . things seem to be fine from where I sit." or "We don't have the capacity to produce 100 additional widgets this year." What do I interpret from these kinds of statements? An inclination toward safety, preservation. In my mind, I call this mental frame "current reality" and allocate the bottom part of the board to these comments.

And, I am curious if this means there is low aspiration in the room. But there are not yet words, data, to confirm this. In my mind, to preserve a place for aspiration, then, I leave an empty area on top of the board for "vision." It's like setting out a plate for a meal that is still being cooked—because the plate is there, the incentive to complete the dish might increase.

As scribes, we frame to offer structure.

The framing in my mind influences the organization of the drawing, which is what others see. What they see influences their understanding of structures in play. Figure 16 in the appendix provides a good example of this, where I used a large timeline to focus attention on the opportunity between what could be and what is, rather than presenting a structure that only focuses on today.

Whether conceptual framing comes easily to you or not, consider it a quick way to structure a board and orient listening. Likewise, if it's easy to see things from one vantage point, consider shifting your view in order to challenge your own frame and the frames of others.

reframe

To reframe is to imagine the same idea from a new view, a new perspective.

We take a notion and turn that notion inside out in order to see it differently, and help others see it differently, thus further opening the door to possibility.

"It's raining out! We need to stay indoors." becomes "The garden is getting watered!" It's not one case or the other; it's both, each supported by a different perspective.

Emotions give us another example. When we feel something strongly—such as sadness in parting with a loved one—we can shift how we relate to that sadness: "I will miss you." can become "I will look forward to being with you again."

If I enter a meeting room as the scribe assuming there will be a clear, smooth surface on which to draw, but instead find flip charts taped on every surface and no open wall area, I have to quickly reframe my approach. I have to find another strategy, such as setting up flip chart easels in a corner or taping paper onto a window. To stay present and carry out the work, I must reconfigure the conditions in my mind. "Full walls" become "Open corners."

Getting fixated within one frame locks us into seeing only one view, whereas being able to reframe allows us to see things from multiple perspectives.

Another tangible example comes from a time when I was asked to scribe at a conference in the oil and gas industry, where there was a focus on fracking (hydraulic fracturing). Considering myself an environmentalist, having intentionally worked with organizations on climate- and species-oriented topics, I thought I knew what I was getting myself into, but then . . .

As I stood on the stage, knowing the drawings would be on display in the main hotel lobby at each break, I questioned what I had done, realizing there was no way out. I'd made a commitment and had to follow through. Presentation after presentation focused on how to increase oil and gas sales, develop local expertise, and increase safety on the rig sites —all to increase investment in fracking. I had a pit in my stomach the entire time. "How can I be supporting any of this?!" I wondered.

However, another part of me knew that in order to serve the room and the client well, I needed to temporarily set aside my personal position. My opposition to fracking did not shift, but I was able to reframe my stance from one that was entirely closed to one that was more open.

And, by raising my level of inquiry, my eyes were also opened. The people in the room were passionate about increasing their business. I am passionate about sustainable energy. Our passions were contrary, but equally strong. As I would want respect for my views, I had to find a way to respect theirs.

In recalling this experience, I realize that a need to reframe can often be linked to strongly held beliefs; the times when I've had to rethink my approach almost always stem from being high on the Ladder of Inference. In order to suspend my beliefs and assumptions, I've had to quickly get a handle on the data being presented and/or work on understanding where other people are coming from.

Getting to the data eases the ability to alter course.

Reframing can facilitate relating. If I can turn something around to see it from your view, I might be able to understand where you're coming from.

As a scribe, by presenting information in a new way—that is, by representing a horizon as an arc rather than as a straight line—I can try to get people on the same page. They have a fresh picture to look at, over which to agree or disagree, and ultimately advance their thinking.

Reframing directly correlates to seeing with fresh eyes.

As soon as we loosen one assumption, we open a window to interpretation and insight.

time

There are three ways I consider time in my work: "over time," "in time," and "right time." I find that content lends itself to different types of presentation in each case. And I find that my stance and approach to a drawing vary once I'm able to recognize how time is implicitly or explicitly being considered by a group or a presenter.

Scribing **over time**, I consider chronology, drawing events in a sequence of past, present, and/or future. Imagine walking *through* a forest, where the surroundings shift as you move along the trail. My drawing might include a timeline (see appendix Figure 16), or I could employ an illustrative style of metaphor to tell the story. This kind of scribing is best suited to the behavioral level of the iceberg.

When scribing **in time**, I represent a fixed idea, and it can serve as a record of one main view. Imagine the expanse from *above* a forest, within which there are visual anchors like treetops, streams, and ponds. To represent a view conceptually, my drawing might include abstract shapes and connectors. Or I could literally recreate the framework someone presents. (See appendix Figures 14 and 15.) This kind of scribing is often suited to the structural and mental model levels of the iceberg.

Right time is where generative scribing comes into play. Time in this sense might be akin to resting *in* a forest and moving naturally only as one is called to move, as spirit or intuition inspire. In this kind of time, which is usually slow and aligned with breath and heartbeat, I might draw a line, or a texture. The form is indicated by the essential feeling of the moment. (See appendix Figure 17.) Generative scribing suits the vision level of the iceberg and works when a group is operating at the level of presencing and source. Awareness of the container and field informs each approach.

By understanding a person or group's view of time, we can more appropriately track and frame what unfolds.

Receiving some advance information from a client about their goals and expectations can facilitate my approach to drawing. If a speaker is recounting a professional journey, I want to use specific words and images to depict that.

If a team is on an annual retreat to explore how to improve their work together, I want to notice dynamics and use shapes and connectors to reveal what is working and what is not (see "The Diamond" chapter in the section "Model of Practice").

If a group is gathered to learn and reflect, then I want to create visual conditions that support their settling into a deeper rhythm by drawing in an open and impressionistic manner.

How we choose to represent time guides how information is received.

Each method of scribing sets the stage for a different interpretation.

A drawing with a beginning and an end, *over time*, implies transition and suggests change. This idea might be unsettling, depending on where a person is positioned. Or, the drawing can simply be a factual display of information that helps people make decisions.

04

A fixed drawing, *in time*, can confront people with how they think and how they organize to make things happen. This is a helpful setup for framing and reframing because it provides a snapshot of a dynamic. If a team is stuck, then mapping the disconnects between team members might help them see what isn't working.

Working with *right timing* is a good way to help reinforce trust in a room. It relieves pressure to perform, since there is no set goal, and does not challenge thinking. It provides spaciousness, allowing the scribe to make the social field more visible and preserving sacred space for new insights to come to light. How drawings look is of secondary importance to the tone they convey.

Sometimes these approaches to time are interwoven.

An *over time* case might include some reflection and then end with an *in time* structure. An organization that wants to adapt to a shifting market might roll out a series of workshops for employees. The workshops include time for deeper conversation. And the result is a new organizational structure.

Or, that same organization might have a structure that is no longer working well. They set aside time to renew and rethink what is needed. The outcome is a staged transition to hire and train new talent.

Or, an organization may be about to merge with a larger corporation, at which time most employees will find themselves in a new structure. Adaptation and adjustment take place on an individual level. Each person must come up with a new plan.

In each of these cases, a scribe could map the whole process and visually represent each part of the sequence in a different way, on separate sheets of paper, that fit together as one larger flow. In Figure 6 in the appendix, the left panel maps current thinking "in time," the center panel addresses desired development "over time," and the right panel represents a conversation in "right time."

My impression is that many clients who engage visual practitioners are unaware of how they are thinking about time. It can be a gift from a generative scribe, then, to offer an organization a picture of its system in context—a picture that, in effect, presents its members with some basic options for engaging with their landscape, their forest.

know

I don't demand that all work be a masterpiece.
What I am doing is the right thing for me
—that is what I am and this is living.
It reflects me and I reflect it.

– Louise Nevelson

know

Focus.

Clarify.

Intuit.

Decide.

Extract essence (and eliminate the superfluous).

Weed whack as necessary to carve a path forward.

Put a stake in the ground for truth.

Root.

What is meant to be seen on a page will surface, now or at some point, through some hand, somewhere.

If it's not visible now, then it's not ready to be seen.

anger

I once agreed to substitute for a colleague whose client
was unfamiliar to me and with whom I had no qualitative
relationship in place. The experience was transformative,
in that I got very mad in the moment, but it led to a
professional decision that has stayed with me ever since.

*Anger, an emotional gateway to the energy
of the Warrior archetype, can guide us to
discernment and clarity.*

I found myself in a hotel ballroom full of middle-aged men in
business suits, the upper management of a large consulting
company. My instructions were to "Just make it look good;
we want something 'sexy.'" In my mind, then, we were
already off to a disagreeable start.

My sense of distaste, even anger, stemmed from several factors.
Leading up to the session, I'd had no direct conversation with
the client's team about the program's content, audience, or
intent, or their hope for the role of the graphics. This led to my
assumption (high on the Ladder of Inference) that the drawings
were meant for short-term use on that day only, in that one
room, and needed to be visually impressive as an exhibit.

But I had committed to the work, so there I was. The topic of
the session and what was said are long gone from my memory.
All I remember was one unfortunate moment.

This was in 2005, before smartphones and social media,
and the group was involved in a complicated computer-
based simulation. They took a break while the technicians
set up a machine on every table. When the group came back,
the technology wasn't ready, and the crowd got restless.

The planning team filled the void by handing out Nerf footballs, which are soft but not *that* soft. And then, almost as if following some primal instinct, the group divided in two. More than a hundred men began randomly throwing toy foam footballs across the conference room at each other. It seemed juvenile, fraternal, and kind of unbelievable all at once.

And there I was—at my easel, near my tray with over thirty markers organized by color, trying to prevent my setup from being knocked over—when I got smacked by a ball on the back of the head. No one had targeted me on purpose, but still . . . it was a direct hit, and it was a bit stunning. I was *mad* (but will spare you the expletives that went through my head).

My anger rose like white heat from the gut to the heart, in an instant. I felt invisible, useless, my work and effort inconsequential. Anger was in me and surrounded me. The only positive outcome? Resolve.

I scribbled on a napkin: *never again*. As quickly as the anger rose, something in me sought action. Since I was there in a support role—and a contracted, temporary one at that— my intuition must have informed me to get through the current moment and set myself up for more constructive conditions going forward.

My resolve thickened. On that same napkin, I wrote out a list of irritated demands that, over time, I have turned into a set of principles that guide *all* my work: relate directly with my clients; try to get a sense of the organization's culture, and partner only where I sense cultural alignment; understand the purpose and expectations for an engagement before accepting any project; know a session's environment and design before arriving on site; only work where respect is a shared value; when angry again, refine the principles.

trust

Scribes must trust their own ability, and there must be trust between the scribe and the social participant body.

When people come together for a meeting, there is often a tension between what is commonly understood and what is murky. Some concepts appear with certainty: "The future is ours to define!" But sometimes content swirls, demanding the scribe's patience and a fine-tuned tracking of the speakers' tone, language, and delivery in order to decipher meaning.

For example, once I was in a three-day session, just days after the Brexit vote, when an official in the Scottish government spoke the following words, almost verbatim, in this sequence:

"Why this, and why not something else? We underestimate how difficult it is to invert the way we are working. Being asked to deconstruct your identity, your armor, and asked to be vulnerable . . . requires rooting. We can build capacity to manage anxiety that is being raised in the system. This uniquely brings together the self and the work and you go on an interior journey."

I was not sure what "this" and "something else" referred to, but as he spoke I scribbled furiously in my journal, desperate to accurately track the words and catch the key line. It all seemed incredibly relevant, but I did not trust myself to filter his words through the ear alone.

Afterward, reviewing my notes, I added to the large picture on the wall: "We underestimate how difficult it is to invert," which was the line that turned my heart upside down and seemed to encapsulate the tone of the entire gathering. (See appendix Figure 31.)

Extracting this (or any) gem required attending to the entire span of a what was said, all the while holding fast to the belief that the key point was there and I would come to know it when ready—when I was ready to receive the message and when the message was ready to be received.

Trust exercises itself within the strength of containers, in mutual holding spaces.

I have probably done my most substantial work in truly trusting relationships and environments. I find that the trust in a room correlates directly with the trust of the container, lifting my capacity and establishing a place where disjointed pieces can fall into place.

A dear colleague once reached out with a request to do some work honoring the 20th anniversary of the "Lion King" musical. My immediate reaction was "Not me! Everyone will want drawings with animals and other recognizable characters from the show." I avoided responding and considered how I could gracefully decline.

But my friend—who knows me, my work, and my reluctance to let people down—followed up. She clarified the opportunity: "I trust that you got my message about a day of planning. You know that you would not be drawing cartoons, right?" What she wanted was "precisely what you do for any group or company —capture the spirit and flow of what is going on." And there we have it—literally and between the lines: *trust*.

And indeed, when we met to map out the project, talking it through and spreading Post-it notes on the floor, the dynamic underpinning it appeared in an instant, and the drawing immediately followed. The relational trust had led directly to trust in an outcome.

*Developing trust takes time. It's a muscle.
It's elastic and can easily snap back and
contract with the slightest slip-up.*

Here are some musings from a day when nothing was clear.
They are reminders to a panicking self from a wiser self that
I now see as small ways to build the trust muscle.

Let go of urgency. Increase care. Slow down. Go slowly.
Breathe. Increase patience.

Source. Know this is the foundation. Access it and stay with it.

Become the container. Envelop the entirety of what you can
see—whatever you can perceive. Go broad. Hold.

Scale. Keep the moment in perspective. This drawing is just a
drop in a vast sea of drawings. This day is one day of thousands.

Sense. At the wall, what wants to be drawn? Before making a
mark, envision the mark. If you can't imagine it, don't draw it.
First, deepen the listening.

Seek understanding. You can only represent as much as you
know. Expand the boundary of your model to expand your
sensemaking capacity.

*Trust takes shape through the mind
and hand, but it is primarily a muscle
of the heart.*

When I operate from a genuine place in myself, and hold
the aspiration for others to operate from a genuine place
too, that seems to relax my heart. From there, trust builds.
And then—with insights, joy, struggle, breakthrough
—trust amplifies.

know

balance

A colleague, Lili Xu, once explained an interpretation of her Chinese culture's symbol of yin / yang as acceptance / desire. The symbol is known as a resolving of opposites, representing a philosophy of interconnected equilibrium.

Dark does not exist without light. Death does not exist without birth. A stroke of a pen does not exist without a surface.

This short exchange led me to wonder about the harmony of the unknown, through acceptance (yin), and the known, through the surfacing of desire (yang). Generative scribing can produce and represent this balance for the participant-viewer.

Also, a scribe's drawings stimulate thinking. I wonder, then, does this thinking further prompt desire, a sort of longing for something not yet attained, "out there," to be reached?

Am I merely creating conditions that reinforce further thinking, thus reinforcing only yang energy?

Or am I also creating conditions that can slow down the mind, building in room for relaxation?

What is the structure I am staging, for action and reflection, based on what I draw?

If I preserve a sense of spaciousness, for both the eye and the mind, will that be perceived as "not enough captured," or might it be experienced as a relief, or as something that provides room for thought and insight?

Yin: That which is left untouched on a surface, empty.

What words are said but never make it to the wall? Is it okay not to catch each formula and bullet point of a presentation? When is the scribe standing still at the wall and intentionally nurturing pause?

Yang: That which is activated through the mark.

If I present the participant-audience with a full board, does that oversaturate the known, like a night sky so full of stars that the eye goes toward the brightness and forgets the proportion of the universe?

coherence

Under all distraction and perceived fragmentation lies a coherent whole.

In any moment, under pressure—at a wall ready to draw, or in the midst of an argument with a loved one—when we want desperately to understand, we can try to inquire into an underlying order, asking: How does this make sense?

We need only look into the woods to understand this principle. Once on a "solo journey" to find some stillness in a forest near Hancock, New Hampshire, I remember my awe when I saw a patch of roots, richly entwined with mushrooms and moss and twigs and insects and lichen and leaves and bark and earth.

This patch represented unique, individual pieces of the forest. And, though the pieces could be viewed unto themselves, the arrangement that resulted from their interrelation was intact. There was no separation between the parts; they co-existed harmoniously, in simultaneous decay and growth.

Had I gazed only at the moss, I might have missed the mushroom. Had I only noticed the frenzy of the ants, I might have missed the leaf! Had I held my gaze on the beauty of any one fragment, I would have missed the intricate natural order.

This same quality, between sections of text and lines and shapes, is precisely what I aim to evoke when I scribe. A board or wall, once complete, ideally has the same resonance as a spot in the woods.

Another way to explain coherence was suggested by the physicist David Bohm:

"Ordinary light is called 'incoherent,' which means that it is going in all sorts of directions, and the light waves are not in phase with each other so they don't build up. But the laser produces a very intense beam which is coherent. The light waves build up strength because they are all going in the same direction. This beam can do all sorts of things that ordinary light cannot." [34]

My practice leans toward the spiritual, correlating coherence with a belief in universal oneness. Aikido master Richard Moon explains well what I feel in applying the principle of coherence at the wall:

"When we feel ourselves a part of the universe, we feel where we are in the flow of Creation, we naturally experience a connectedness with the earth. Feeling this connection effortlessly heals the isolation that characterizes modern life. Life becomes connectedness and we find ourselves in empowered alignment with the universe as it unfolds." [35]

---

34 David Bohm, *On Dialogue*, edited by Lee Nichol (London: Routledge, 1996), p. 14.

35 Richard Moon, *Aikido in Three Easy Lessons* (San Rafael, CA: Aiki Press, 1996), p. 49.

In applying this principle of coherence at the wall, sometimes I will draw a large curve or shape, seemingly out of nowhere. No one in the room has said "And it all starts with a large arc." But as I think about intertwined nature in the woods, I know the arc will fit with other blocks of words (like rocks) and texture (like moss). I know it will all hold together in the end.

I quiet my rambling mind, look at and into the wall, and have a quick conversation with that surface: "What is your story today? What wants to be revealed on your big, blank surface?" Obviously the wall does not talk back. But in a way it does. I receive some sort of impulse to exercise a certain gesture, go in a particular direction, even choose a specific color. And I go from there.

I trust that the first mark will fit with all the marks to come, that the gesture is originating from some deep unseen place of aligned intent—like a laser infused with a creative urge— and, through my hand, will manifest as shapes on the wall that make cognitive and aesthetic sense. (See appendix Figure 18.)

There is a similar trusting to be found in conversation.

If I find myself amped up and ranting about how someone is irritating me or offending me, latching onto the face value of the exchange, the me-them polarity, will reinforce the fragmentation. Instead, seeking the coherence in the situation can increase compassion and development. Keeping the following question in mind usually—not always!—helps me settle down: "How and why are these things playing out in this way, at this time?"

Putting ourselves in someone else's shoes is a first step toward becoming aware of where they are coming from. Trying to see the entire exchange from above can enhance my perspective.

And seeking sense in the underlying root causes can
further expand my comprehension.

*To discern any one fragment, first imagine
and believe in a larger, more entwined,
interconnected picture.*

If I draw isolated elements, it's as if I'm displaying an
arrangement of rocks collected from various places.
They're beautiful, and they are dismembered from
their original context.

In generative scribing, we recontextualize elements all the
time, and that is precisely where coherence can aid us.
We can reorder content with our will and impose structure;
and/or we can inquire into a natural, whole, emerging state
that is seeking new form.

Seeking coherence demands a lot *of trust.*

Whether we are drawing a picture on a wall or having an
awkward conversation with a co-worker, trust encourages us
to consider that this picture or that conversation is exactly what
is meant to unfold in a particular window of time. It's simply a
piece of the greater context, still becoming known.

discernment

TRANSFORM

ENGAGE

BYPASS

NAME

ATTENUATE   AMPLIFY

Scribes have to choose what to do with the steady stream of content we hear behind our heads. Part of choosing what to draw is subjective, based on our listening skills; part is objective, based on our ability to order and sift data; and part is generative, based on how we connect with source.

One framework, Bypass-Name-Engage-Transform, has proven very useful for managing large amounts of information, helping me decide what and when to draw.[36] Note that these four actions do not happen in linear sequence; all four happen at once in a continual and fluid process of "letting go" in order to "let come," as we experience in presencing. Here is a breakdown of how I apply the four components of this framework.

36 The original framework was conceived by Diana McLain Smith, "Choose the Right Strategy," in *Divide or Conquer: How Great Teams Turn Conflict into Strength* (New York: Portfolio/Penguin Group, 2008), p. 177. It was then adapted by William Isaacs in the context of dialogic leadership.

generative scribing

In the context of generative scribing, to Bypass is to intentionally not draw.

As a way of tracking the overall flow of a presentation or its content, we resist the urge to write something down until it is clear how the idea fits into the developing picture.

Not everything that is spoken needs to be translated onto the wall. As I describe in the chapter "Choice," this is where we ease tension for ourselves by accepting that if we understand some of the bits, that is enough.

We choose to focus on the parts that make sense to us— logically and/or intuitively—and surrender the rest. We also deepen our inquiry and attend to the container in order to recognize what is actually needed for the social body to see.

To Name is to choose to include information in the picture.

We might note something of interest in our mind, on a Post-it, or scribbled on the side of a panel. If we draw, it's literal, using specific words and images that accurately map the speaker's language and intent.

Sometimes to name is to simply make a list. Seeing key points might be all the group needs to stay on track, and to further interpret meaning at this stage would not be appropriate.

Container sensitivity is key. It's helpful to know where a group is, where they are trying to go, and how much they want to see or can handle seeing in the moment.

When naming, I keep an ear open to content repetition, reinforcement, and differentiation. I notice, to myself: "What is the same? What stands out?"

05

To Engage is to bring patterns to light, to deepen inquiry, and to expand the container.

When a point comes up repeatedly, I make sure to include it. I listen from the perspective of the speaker(s), the system, and the social field to recognize unclear verbal streams, with the goal of uncovering the essence of what someone —or a group—is trying to express. (See appendix Figure 19.)

Considering the iceberg model, I seek to identify some structure that's guiding the expression or interaction. I want to figure out what is influencing the mindset of the person speaking. What are the speakers trying to influence with their words?

A group on the verge of breakdown, for example, about to devolve into arguments, might be pushed over the edge by a hastily drawn list that tracks points of opposition. Or maybe this is exactly what they need to break through to different thinking! Explore what is at risk, what is not being said, and what might be seeking expression.

Note that engaging requires a higher degree of skill than purely naming. Graphic recording, which is mirroring content in a literal manner, would be naming. Graphic facilitation, which demands that the practitioner participate in a group's process, would be engaging. To engage is to connect themes within a picture and across the people in a room.

To Transform is to make choices, and moves, that support a shift in individual, group, and system dynamics.

Even from the side of the room we have influence to either disrupt or stabilize through our drawing. Transform with care!

Listen deeply to space between the words for what wants to be seen. Trust that a deeper meaning will arrive, and be ready to include it. And if nothing comes, nothing is yet meant to come.

Notice the sequence and the flow of voices as well as other sounds coming into the room. Once a small flock of starlings darted to and fro, just outside an open window, inches from the end of my wall-long drawing. Their movements and chirps were at first distracting. I named their presence, in my mind, but chose to bypass and keep going.

I had never witnessed such seemingly random flight patterns, though, and that intrigued me. The birds held my attention, so I decided to engage their activity. I drew them in around the words someone spoke—"I want to feed myself"—which, through the process in the room, had come to symbolize self-actualizing. This was the transformative mark.

As generative scribes, we can also influence a room by either increasing or decreasing awareness of certain content, turning up or down the volume.

If an idea has already been expressed several times, we can reinforce it by writing it repeatedly (amplifying). Or we can decide to balance the idea within the overall content of the picture by including just a few keywords (attenuating).

Depending on the needs of a group, we can use a synthetic approach, taking in lots of content and organizing it into clusters, carefully framing and making connections, reducing the complexity and offering cohesion. The resulting image is highly integrated across one plane, one piece of paper.

We could also choose to use a deconstructive approach, intentionally taking one concept and breaking it into parts, so that what seems like a knot becomes easier to untangle. The resulting image would be the opposite of cohesive, as the approach aims to extract ideas—to expand a conversation and prompt new thinking.

Either approach—balancing or reinforcing—can be woven into any phase of Bypass-Name-Engage-Transform.

As we make sense of what we hear and what is called for in the room, we can actively choose how to respond.

I consider the Know domain to be as informed by the internal and even spiritual senses as it is by any rational thinking.

Content floats, my being moves in and out of it. When something lands in my heart or buzzes louder in my head, and my body cannot *not* act on that signal, then I draw.

choice

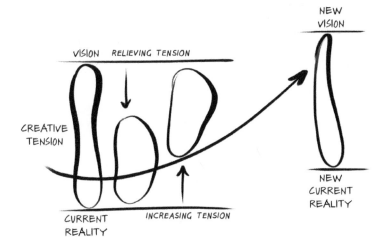

VISION RELIEVING TENSION

CREATIVE
TENSION

CURRENT
REALITY

INCREASING TENSION

NEW
VISION

NEW
CURRENT
REALITY

In life and in facilitation, the ability to manage creative tension
can mean the difference between growing or collapsing.

With vision above and reality at the base, creativity resides
between the two. This model from Robert Fritz shows how
a practice can remain static or be stretched.[37] "Tension seeks
resolution" he writes. We are hungry. We eat.

In our practice, we determine the amount of tension we want to sustain.

Sometimes I can determine the structure of my working
environment, such as where to set up in a room or choosing
who is on my team. At other times elements of the structure
are determined for me, like being required to use the colors
of a company's logo or to draw in a particular style.

37 Robert Fritz, *Creating: a Guide to the Creative Process* (New York:
    Fawcett Columbine, 1991), p. 27.

In defining my own structure, when do I challenge myself in order to move into my desired future, raising my own bar? Or, when do I accept a limit in order to ease some pressure? The answer depends on the nature of the creative tension in my mind (dread or excitement), in my heart (lump of sadness or joy), and in my body (stomach in knots or raring to go).

A wide gap between an aspiration and current reality indicates a high level of tension. Noticing this, I ask myself: "How much can I take? Can my and the group's container hold a higher-keyed energy? Where are others in their level of comfort or stress? Can the system expand its boundaries?"

Scribes draw to either relieve or increase tension, and thus facilitate the pace of change in conversation.

Sometimes a group seems edgy, unstable. I will probably want to help hold things together and touch an underlying order to minimize tension. I get more grounded in data to understand how the bits of content fit together to make sense. I imagine the social body as an organism seeking some quiet, rest. I draw more slowly, more carefully. I soften my stance, listen more deeply, and relate to what needs more time to resolve.

Sometimes a group seems ripe for movement. So I draw with more speed, more conviction. My attitude is that possibility is within reach. My marks come out crisp, steady, as if carving a direction for the group to gain momentum and courage.

Over time, if a group intends to change, a generative scribe can help raise the level of vision and note the updated current reality. With attunement to where a group has been and where they aspire to go, we can make the path visible. We can set up conditions for choice.

draw

Making your unknown known is the important thing—and keeping the unknown always beyond you—catching— crystallizing your simpler clearer vision of life—only to see it turn stale compared to what you vaguely feel ahead—that you must always keep working to grasp...

– Georgia O'Keeffe

draw

To draw is to practice, to manifest.

This is the domain in which we make things happen. This is
where we take all that we have cultivated in our interior realm
and do something with it. This is where we make things visible
for ourselves and others. This is the tip of the iceberg, the seen.

We draw through the hand, yes, and we draw informed by the
interior spectrum of activity—our core being—how we have
joined, how we perceive, and how we have come to know.

What is seen, what is witnessed in form by ourselves and
others, is a pure expression of the complete processing of
information across the inner and outer range. We visually
reflect conditions of the moment based on our ability to
contain, to hold, the suite of complexities we witness.

Drawing is a synthesis, an orchestration, a weaving together
of inputs from the entire range below the iceberg's water line:
the social field, mindsets, structural dynamics, and behaviors.

And through our drawing we meet the potential to reveal
a current state of events and also future possibilities. Thus,
through our drawing we have a power—and therefore a true
responsibility—to represent the possible and help initiate it
into the present moment.

Scribing is, in a way, like midwifing; it helps the unborn to birth,
bringing to life a new reality.

joy

Through joy, I access the doorway to creating.

Joy comes in all shapes and sizes; even a small grain of it
can free my will into motion.

Joy is the feeling that comes with "They get it . . .
It makes sense to people! They understand! I helped them see!"

Joy is watching a little kid in an audience come up to the wall,
point at something in the drawing, and drop his jaw at what he
has encountered.

Joy is sending an image to my dad and, even if he doesn't
completely understand what I do, having him tear up with
pride that his daughter has done something like this
(whatever "this" is . . . it doesn't matter.)

Joy is receiving support from the people I love.

Joy is waking up excited to start the day.

Joy is noticing a small leaf, appreciating its color, trying to
create that color with dry-erase inks, and seeing that leaf come
to life on the wall. (See appendix Figures 20 and 21.)

Joy is knowing the color of the leaf intimately, even if no one
else on the planet knows why I mixed that specific color, even
if no one in the room or on the planet knows that color comes
from a little leaf.

Joy is "this color is so bleeping beautiful I could draw with it
my entire life."

Joy is letting go of the need for an elephant to look like an elephant and simply enjoying the effort of making a dangling trunk by drawing a curved line.

Joy is using a drill and a clamp to extract ink from chalk markers and fill a small Mason jar, and being able to brush that chalk ink onto a decades-old piece of slate.

Joy is walking into a room and seeing a circle of forty chairs, empty, waiting.

Joy is even exhaustion, on a flight home after sleepless nights, with an aching arm and a saturated mind, knowing that I had some small part in helping something larger to shift.

Joy is personal, often found in small, unnoticed places: cracks in sidewalks, abandoned yards, scurrying ants, a tide sweeping in and covering sand only to withdraw and leave small, glistening pebbles.

Joy is witnessing people as they are moved and enter a new state of being, the beauty of human growth, the sheer, absolute, beauty of humanity.

envisioning

Envisioning works closely with coherence, as it is a way of tapping into an existing, underlying order of things and bringing aspects of that forward.

Oftentimes—almost every time—before a session, I am nervous and uncertain. "Will what I make live up to the standards of the client, of the profession? Will the drawings serve any purpose? Will anyone even notice them?"

To calm my nerves, years ago I developed an almost superstitious process that I use to this day. I call it: "Walking in Grandma's shoes."

My grandmother Claire Nichtern could always cut through to the core of things, with attitude, or in Yiddish, *chutzpah*. She rose from immigrant poverty to produce musicals on Broadway, and when my brother and I were little she would take us to opening nights. We would hang onto her hands as she led us to the prime, reserved, fifth-row aisle seats.

She seemed to know everyone, and knew her place in the arrangement of things. She knew who was sitting where, who was acting in the play, who was having an affair, who had written the music, who had been let go at the last minute.

As a producer, she understood the makings of a successful show, and that came with a certain confidence and air of power.

I never had a conversation with her about this quality, and am not sure how genuine or projected it was. But what I do know is that I step into that place of imagined success when I need to beef up my own ability to pull a positive outcome closer.

At some point on the morning of a session, when I am
nervous and jittery, between leaving my hotel room and
arriving in front of a wall, I take a few steps and envision
walking in her (custom-molded-for-her-bad-back and
looking-as-if-they-were-designed-for-moon-walking) shoes.
Very solid shoes that knew exactly where they were going.

I then start to play out the day in my mind, as if predicting
the sequence of actions: walk to breakfast and eat the fruit
(when I really want the muffin). Lay out the markers on
the table or ledge, all ink-filled, poised. Stand tall and calm,
connected to earth and sky. Mind alert, tuned in to the
moment, focused. Sections of content holding together in an
organized manner. Board complete and accurately reflecting
what I heard, what I sensed.

All this envisioning, all before lifting a pen.

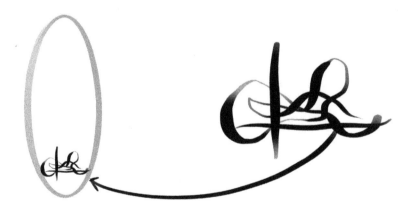

levels of scribing

There exist depths, or phases, of scribing that directly correlate with attention.

Different "levels" of listening can help us participate in a shift of awareness and possibility. Otto Scharmer has described four levels of listening: (1) downloading; (2) factual listening; (3) empathic listening; and (4) generative listening.[38] I apply each level of listening to the visual practice of scribing, as depicted here.

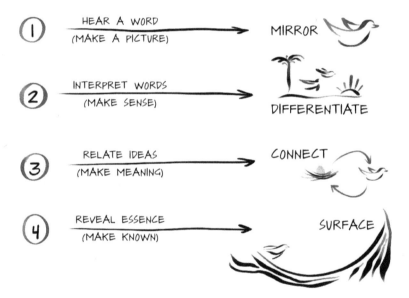

① HEAR A WORD
(MAKE A PICTURE) ⟶ MIRROR

② INTERPRET WORDS
(MAKE SENSE) ⟶ DIFFERENTIATE

③ RELATE IDEAS
(MAKE MEANING) ⟶ CONNECT

④ REVEAL ESSENCE
(MAKE KNOWN) ⟶ SURFACE

generative scribing

38 C. Otto Scharmer, *Theory U: Leading from the Future as It Emerges*
(San Francisco: Berrett-Koehler, 2009), Introduction.

Level one scribing: Mirror.
We hear a word and make a picture.

We use level one listening, "downloading," to reconfirm and reflect what we already know.

Our drawing is literal; someone says "bird" and we draw a bird. I also refer to this as "object-oriented" scribing, where a focus on individual, named parts is the primary approach. We track largely at a data level, naming the literal words, and draw in areas on a page in a somewhat isolated manner.

Level two scribing: Differentiate.
We interpret words and make sense.

We use level two listening, "factual listening," to notice differences and data that disconfirm what we think we already know.

In scribing, we interpret what is being spoken from a broader vantage point. We still draw what we hear, but our lens expands to make sense of what is being said in a factual context, which we can diagram. The bird is flying; then it reaches the coast and joins a flock. At this level we enter the domain of storytelling. We might draw the literal scene, or mind map to organize data into information.

Level three scribing: Connect.
We relate ideas and make meaning.

We use level three listening, "empathic listening," to see a situation through the eyes of another, to make an emotional connection. We get out of our own skin, step back, and get added perspective that helps us direct our attention to the entirety of a person or situation.

06

This is where containers are activated, where our own heart comes online, where we feel. We start to care, genuinely care, and our stance shifts. Our drawing shifts (how can it not?!) as it comes, literally, from a deeper place in our body. Not only the head and the hand are in motion, but the entire torso is engaged in our output.

We realize the story in the room is coming from a cultural frame of reference beyond the room; the facts coming out have causal underpinning. No bird, no story, exists as an island. Something came before the lone bird flying, and something will come after. We could connect the scenes of (1) a lone bird flying with (2) a bird reaching the coast—and by establishing that relation show the bird's path.

We shift from noticing moments in time to sensing movements over time. As we inquire, we start to inhabit the story and make sense of it on an expanded scale. What happens between the bird taking flight and the bird landing? What was the bird's behavior along the way? What influences, such as weather or predators, did it encounter?

Level four scribing: Surface. We reveal what wants to be seen.

Using level four listening, "generative listening," we connect with our capacity to let go and let come an emerging future possibility that reveals more fully who we are and who we want to be.

In level four, or generative, scribing we sense and uncover the highest potentiality for the systems we serve. This requires being sensitive not only to the content that is obvious and clear, but also to the content that is fuzzy, blurred, faint—small tones of hesitancy in a speaker's voice, long pauses between words, coughing that subtly interrupts a sentence.

In level four scribing, we connect with source, and with social and energetic fields. We listen to voices in the room. We *also* have our full selves open and receptive to all kinds of sensory and intuitive inputs: rain on the roof, a fly buzzing around someone's juice cup, the freshness or staleness of the air, the quality of being of the presenter and other participants (at ease, jittery, highly focused . . .), the light, the shadows —a sort of pulse in the air.

Here we might inquire into the space around the bird along its entire path. Why is it flying alone? Is it seeking its flock? Where will the flock go next? Will it stay intact? What is the season? What is its health?

To understand how to apply these levels more concretely, simply replace "bird" with "business plan," "flying" with "management process," "coast" with "quarterly profits," "flock" with "strategic plan," "predators" with "competition," "weather" with "economic climate," and "calling" with "vision." And then imagine what drawing or facilitating those aspects of a conversation would be like.

Match the level of scribing to the needs of the situation.

I would not show up for a summer picnic wearing a down jacket and carrying snowshoes. Likewise, I would not expect to exercise generative scribing in a thirty-minute introduction, where three people had eight minutes each to set up their content expertise. Different settings require different approaches. And each level of scribing has a value and relevant application.

Level one scribing is great for conferences where presentations are short and multiple people share their thoughts in bursts. (See appendix Figure 22.)

Level two scribing is useful for panel discussions, academic lectures, negotiations, strategic planning, even system mapping. (See appendix Figure 23.)

Level three scribing is relational, emphasizing the interaction between elements. It's a useful approach in storytelling, dialogue, culture mapping. (See appendix Figure 24.)

And with level four scribing, as in appendix Figure 25, we draw what must be drawn in the developing reality, representing the absolute present moment as it unfolds, in right time. It's useful in ongoing large-scale change initiatives, cross-sector and multi-stakeholder settings, contexts of societal transformation.

generative scribing

Generative scribing is a drawing process with which we open to the unknown to bring it to life—of, and for, a social body.

My experience with this kind of work, where we operate from source, leads me to believe that the key to generative scribing is sensing from the heart.

It's not circling or hovering. It's not counting the minutes until a person stops speaking and we can go home. It's not staying comfortable with me-them. It's not *not* caring.

It is piercing through to something essential. Seeing clearly without fear of the result or consequence of what comes forward. It requires trust in the complete blankness of things. It can only happen when the social body (a handful or thousands of people) is committed to being together in place and time—and in right timing—committed to joining in the absolute present moment. (See appendix Figure 26.)

It's groping in the dark to find threads of hope, and getting that out and up on a wall for others to see.

It's believing that anyone who witnesses the drawing is an active participant in its creation. There is no "other."

There is a hand that holds a marker, that leans forward from the extended arm of an upright physical body acting purely on behalf of the whole.

I draw because we exist; I draw as a social act.

Generative scribing is drawing to ease the challenge of societal inversion, where we are shifting from a state of division to a state of inclusion, traversing an unknown.

I have often wondered—especially in light of symbolic art, such as that of indigenous peoples—about the true potential of scribing to cross physical and spiritual lines.

Can a scribed image embody the dimensionality of past, present, and future in a larger timelessness, all at once?

How far can we push the comprehensive limits of systems, and our own limits, to shift the place of understanding between known and unknown worlds? Can scribing generate a vibrational field that goes beyond literal words and transcends the moment?

To date, to attempt to shift into this space, I have taken an integrative approach to revealing unnamed wholeness; I've synthesized multiple threads of content into one encapsulating picture, or a series of pictures. In a way it's the opposite of storytelling, which I have interpreted as the sharing of existing data in linear flow.

Once when I approached three very large, looming, black banners of blank paper, I recalled a similar sensation of darkness, of uncertainty. (See appendix Figure 27.)

It was tied to a memory from a night sailing on the ocean with my dad and brother. We had charts, but there was no land in sight—just cold rolling waters, an impenetrable indigo through which the boat somehow cut. For a few hours, or maybe it was only one hour, we had no radio and no indication of whether storms or other vessels were headed our way.

But my dad, having navigated for years in all kinds of weather and water, has always been confident in his ability to read the conditions and guide a boat. That night—aside from a close encounter with a fishing vessel, which we approached more out of curiosity than in lost wandering—we were, indeed, fine.

Generative scribes aid with societal tacking.

As a verb, "to tack" is "to change course by turning a boat's head into and through the wind." As a noun, "tack" is "a small, sharp, broad-headed nail" and "a long stitch used to fasten fabrics together temporarily, prior to permanent sewing." All of these meanings make sense in scribing! Scribed images can inform a redirection in corporate strategy (changing course), land a point with precise language (as a nail), and hold ideas together as they take shape (fasten).

As our society rolls in and out of foggy waters, scribes can help chart the seas.

Scribes create visual structures that aid in navigating disconnects. In doing so, we balance the challenges of the times with hope for our times. (See appendix Figure 28.)

This demands constant fluidity between sensing, comprehending, and crafting. Before drawing, I center myself. I find someone in the audience and look them in the eye to activate my heart. I question the structure and dynamics of the setting. I absorb many words before knowing which ones are the pearls and emptying those onto a two-dimensional plane.

We listen to empathize and to represent.

It is with a continually swaying spirit—between what is and what could be—that I draw, that I write.

And, with a far-flung aspiration, I encourage anyone who has reached this point in the book to take on the challenge and transformational gifts that generative scribing has to offer. If your craft or practice is something other than scribing, then you can apply a generative approach to that too!

My experience is just a starting point. It's our opportunity, together, to further define this art form and tap its full possibility.

the call

"Our time is a time for crossing barriers,
for erasing old categories—for probing around."

—Marshall McLuhan

It is astounding to think about where scribing is today,
as a practice, when it did not even exist just forty years ago.
When I first got involved in 1995, it was before digital cameras,
America Online and the Internet were just taking off, and the
only way to share drawings with others remotely was through
an elaborate process of redrawing, photocopying,
and distributing copies by hand or post.

Knowing how much this practice has transformed over the
past few decades, I can only imagine what the future will
hold for scribing, and for generative scribing—forty, twenty,
even five years out.

Will generative scribing, which comes to
life through a mix of intuition and social
context, be one art-based answer to
preserving the human spirit?

When artificial intelligence has the ability—and superior
acumen—to visually map a conversation, where will the
human capacity fit in? How will scribes need to adapt their
current methods, which will be increasingly challenged by
technical permeation and by more diffused distribution?

Certainly there will be shifts having to do with time and
distance. We already can draw digitally and project images
onto mega-screens during conferences. And we can work
remotely, using a tablet to live-stream our drawing into an
online video meeting.

I think there will soon be more co-creation across time zones and between locations. I will be working on one image in one place, and someone else will be working on another image in another place. But the level of integration will increase.

Maybe we will work on the same image at once, or maybe our two images will simultaneously display side-by-side in another location. There will undoubtedly be new complexities to consider when the practice shifts beyond a place-based effort that is contained in one room, in one slice of time.

I wonder what will happen when both the number of scribes and the number of people in the participant-audience increase. Right now one person draws for many people. It is still usually through one person's hand that an image is crafted.

What will happen when more people can create an image at once? What if a hundred or a thousand people could visually contribute to one drawing simultaneously, the way they now provide input via a hashtag to a Twitter stream?

How will the visual maintain its aesthetic coherence? How will sensemaking occur, when multiple inputs lead to a data blitz?

I have no idea about the mechanics of this. But I do predict that the level of field activation will increase and thus will require an expanded container to hold the amplified energy.

Generative scribes will be called to expand our consciousness and deepen our capacity.

Generative scribing as we know it today—of the field, through one hand, for the field—will remain just that, or it will progress with the times to serve an evolving social field. As our species advances and expands its consciousness (and I trust it will), generative scribing, a burgeoning art form, will follow suit.

***If generative scribing is a participatory art,
then the nature of its creation will change
along with changes in the social field.***

We need people—of all ages and from all places—to take this
practice into the streets and merge it with other art forms, to
take it beyond corporate and organizational environments,
to take it into parts of society where money doesn't determine
where creativity can flourish, to grow this practice so that
visual communication becomes as commonplace as writing
a sentence or talking with a friend.

Since this is a visual medium, the more people who experience
generative scribing—as makers, as part of the social fabric that
requires the making—the more room and call there will be for
invention and improvement of our methods.

With the fervent hope that we will increase our ability to see,
meet the complexity of our times, and break through to a more
harmonic way of co-existing with ourselves and our planet,
I issue this plea: to expand the true potential of this unique art
and its practice, and to serve our species, look inward.

appendix

Figure 1: *Scribing.* Demonstration of the zone that forms between scribe, speaker, and participant-audience at a session of the World Economic Forum in Nuevo Vallarta, Mexico. Permanent ink on a custom-built wall, 7'h x 40'w, 2012. Photo credit: Alfredo Carlo.

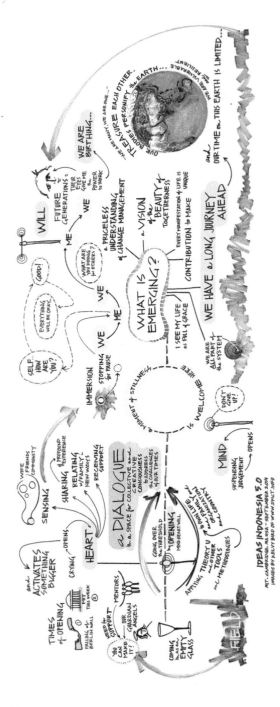

Figure 2: *Integration.* This drawing mapped a two-hour dialogue at the end of a year-long leadership program. It demonstrates the application of system dynamics and balancing voices in the room. Cambridge, MA, USA. Dry-erase ink on whiteboard, 4'h x 12'w, 2014.

Figure 3: *Integration.* Example of flow coming into the room through multiple voices, and weaving individual contributions into one thread. "We have a long journey ahead . . ." "and our time . . . " "we are vulnerable . . . " "treasure each other."

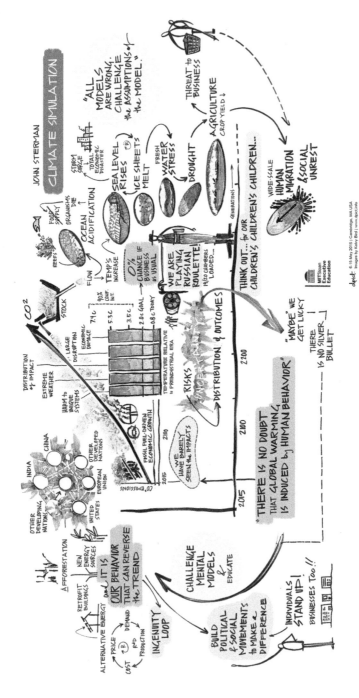

Figure 4: *The Iceberg.* As applied to scribing for a C-ROADS Climate Simulation led by John Sterman, director of the MIT System Dynamics Group, Cambridge, MA, USA. Dry-erase ink on whiteboard, 4'h x 8'w, 2015.

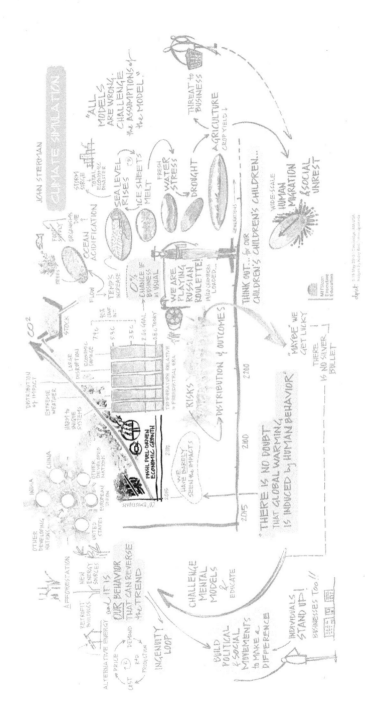

Figure 5: *The Iceberg: Structures.* Detail from Figure 4. This part of the wall mapped some of the structures that create climate change.

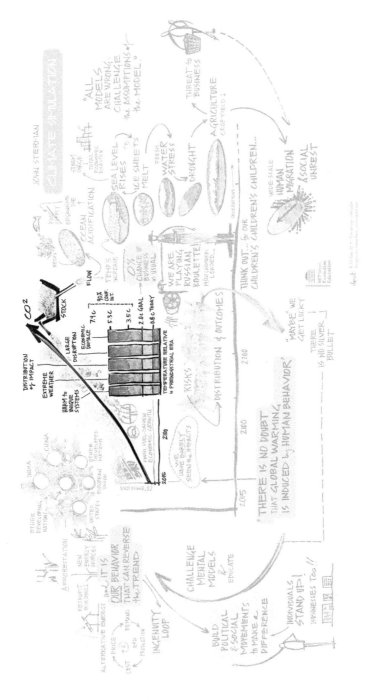

Figure 6: *The Iceberg: Patterns of Behavior.* Detail from Figure 4. This part of the wall mapped current and projected global warming trends.

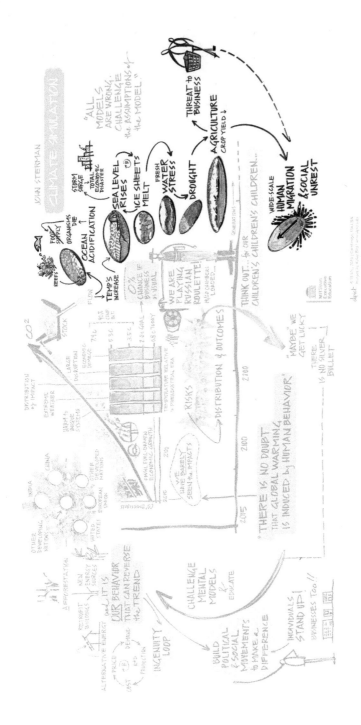

Figure 7: *The Iceberg: Events.* Detail from Figure 4. This part of the wall mapped current and future scenarios.

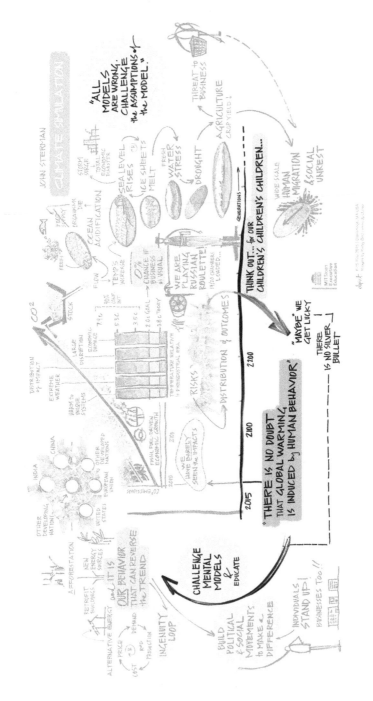

Figure 8: *The Iceberg: Mental Models.* Detail from Figure 4. This part of the wall mapped how our thinking could change to redirect future outcomes.

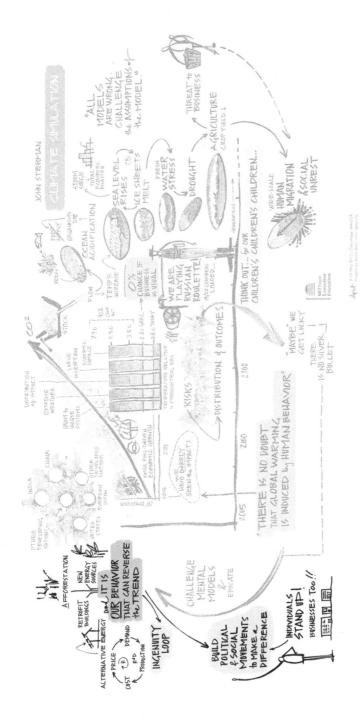

Figure 9: *The Iceberg: Vision*. Detail from Figure 4. This part of the wall envisioned tangible actions that could create a desired future.

Figure 10: *Containers*. A final circle led by Arawana Hayashi during the Presencing Masterclass, with the drawing on the far wall. Berlin, Germany. 2012.

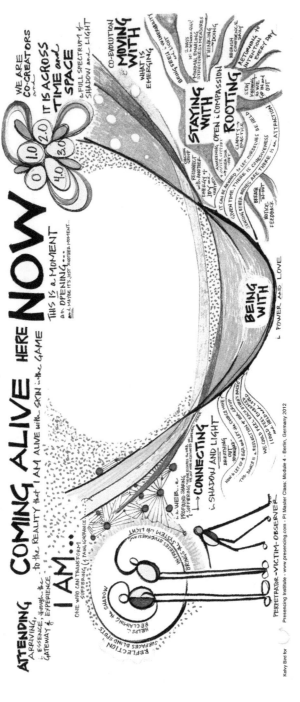

Figure 11: *Presencing.* Detail from the masterclass drawing, where I first became aware of presencing entering the room and the picture simultaneously. Permanent ink on paper, 2012.

Figure 12: *Authenticity.* It's not always pretty, but it's real! To conserve energy, my effort now goes into the gestures I use to apply my marks, before striving for literal accuracy. Dry-erase ink on whiteboard, 2017.

Figure 13: *Listening.* Using a headset for translation from Mandarin into English, during a workshop demonstration in Taipei, Taiwan. Permanent ink on paper, 2016. Photo credit: Tsunami Lin.

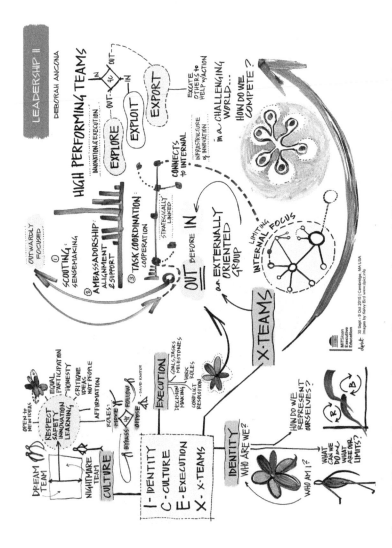

Figure 14: *In Time.* Here is an approach to recording one main framework, "X-Teams," as presented by Deborah Ancona of the MIT Leadership Center. Cambridge, MA, USA. Dry-erase ink on whiteboard, 4'h x 5'w, 2015.

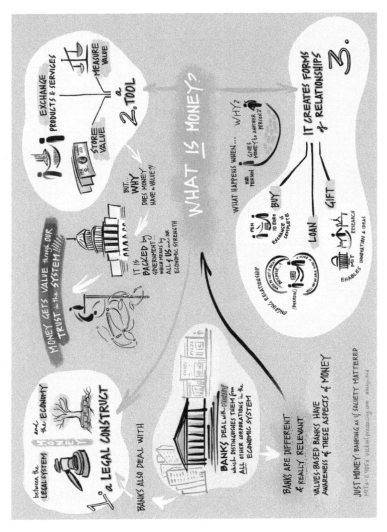

Figure 15: *In Time.* This example describes the concept of money, for the online EdX mooc: Just Money: Banking As If Society Matters, iPadPro using ProCreate, 2016.

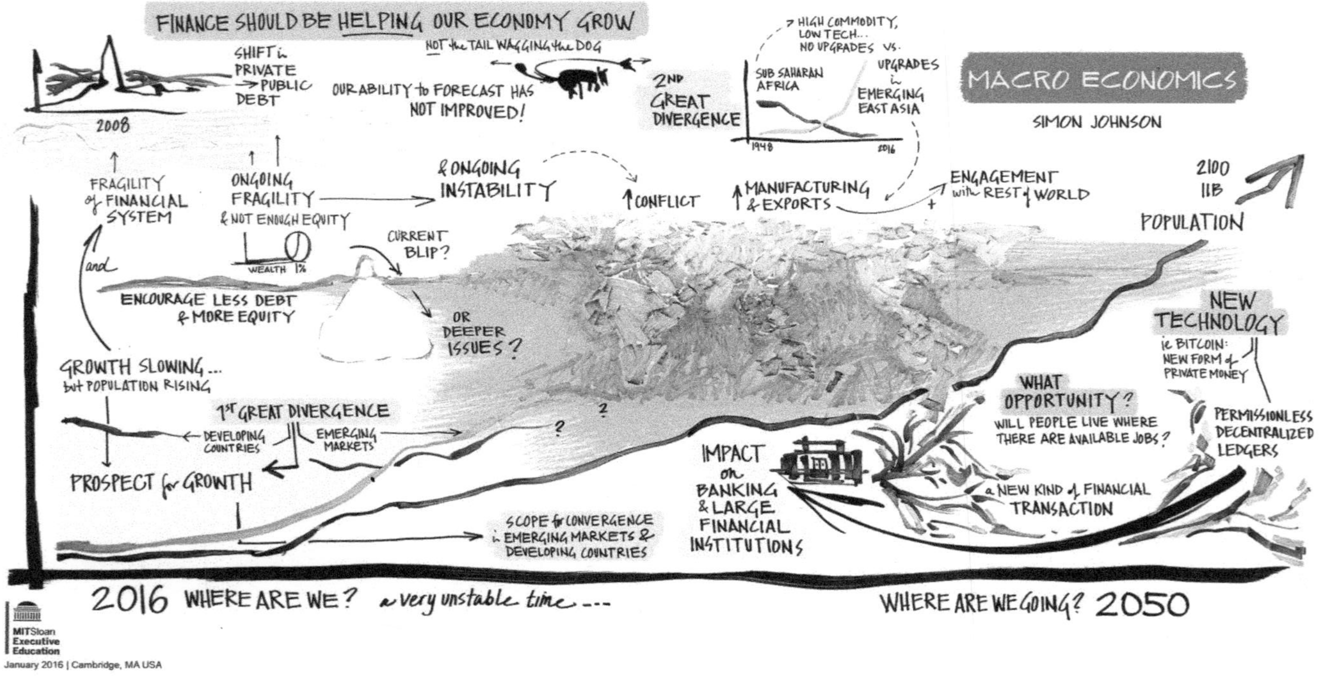
FINANCE SHOULD BE HELPING OUR ECONOMY GROW
2008
SHIFT in PRIVATE → PUBLIC DEBT
NOT the TAIL WAGGING the DOG
OUR ABILITY to FORECAST HAS NOT IMPROVED!
2ND GREAT DIVERGENCE
HIGH COMMODITY, LOW TECH... NO UPGRADES vs.
SUB SAHARAN AFRICA
UPGRADES in EMERGING EAST ASIA
1948
2016
MACRO ECONOMICS
SIMON JOHNSON
FRAGILITY of FINANCIAL SYSTEM
ONGOING FRAGILITY
& NOT ENOUGH EQUITY
WEALTH 1%
& ONGOING INSTABILITY
CONFLICT
MANUFACTURING & EXPORTS
ENGAGEMENT with REST of WORLD
2100
11B
POPULATION
and
CURRENT BLIP?
ENCOURAGE LESS DEBT & MORE EQUITY
OR DEEPER ISSUES?
NEW TECHNOLOGY
ie BITCOIN: NEW FORM of PRIVATE MONEY
GROWTH SLOWING... but POPULATION RISING
WHAT OPPORTUNITY?
WILL PEOPLE LIVE WHERE THERE ARE AVAILABLE JOBS?
1ST GREAT DIVERGENCE
DEVELOPING COUNTRIES
EMERGING MARKETS
PERMISSIONLESS DECENTRALIZED LEDGERS
IMPACT on BANKING & LARGE FINANCIAL INSTITUTIONS
PROSPECT for GROWTH
a NEW KIND of FINANCIAL TRANSACTION
SCOPE for CONVERGENCE in EMERGING MARKETS & DEVELOPING COUNTRIES
2016 WHERE ARE WE? a very unstable time ---
WHERE ARE WE GOING? 2050
MITSloan Executive Education
January 2016 | Cambridge, MA USA

Figure 16: *Over Time.* Here I used a timeline to map a talk by Simon Johnson, professor of entrepreneurship at the MIT Sloan School of Management, on macroeconomics over a thirty-year span. Dry-erase ink on whiteboard, 4'h x 8'w, 2014. (See full wall in Figure 33.)

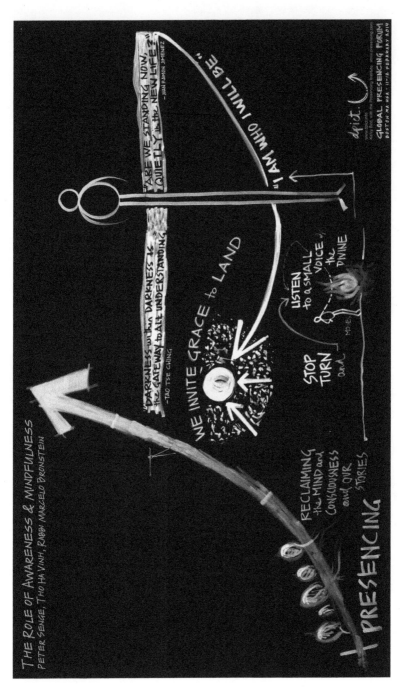

Figure 17: *Right Time.* A detail from Figure 18, showing the minimal drawing approach that captured three speakers' content on mindfulness.

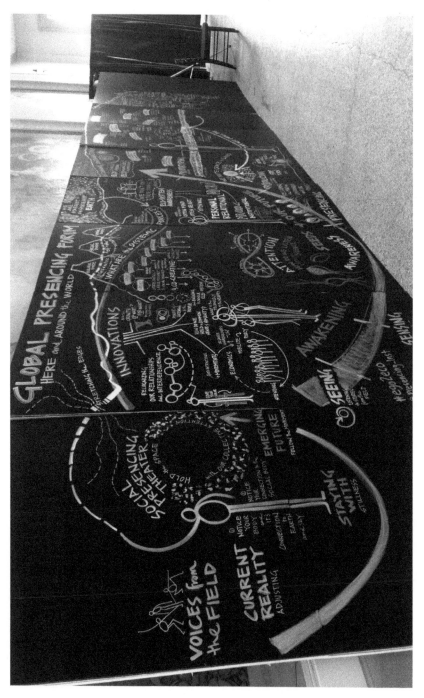

Figure 18: *Coherence.* For a three-day gathering of about 250 people, I wove all plenary content into this one long wall. It came together to form a strange mammal, which I did not intend (but loved). See the eye and tusk on the far left. Acrylic paint on foam board, 5'h x 30'w, 2014.

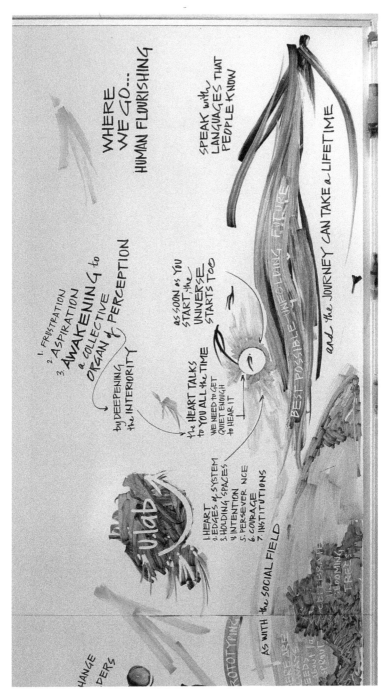

Figure 19: *Discern.* An example of engaging a key message pertaining to the "best possible emerging future." The lines of the large, gestural arrow, and the bird in the empty circle with gold around it, demonstrate an effort to "transform" that same message. Dry-erase ink on whiteboard, 2016.

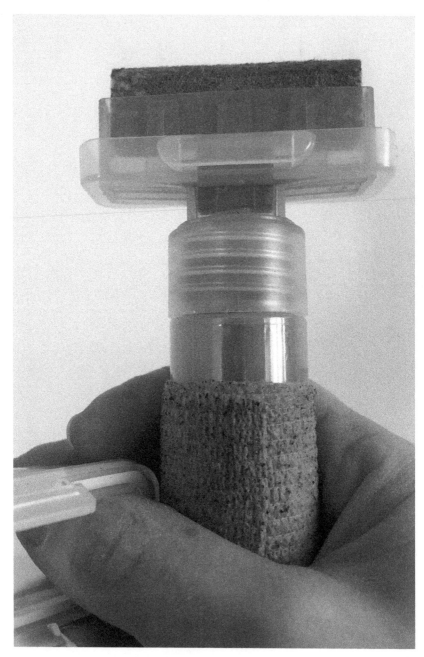

Figure 20: *Joy.* Custom-mixed Neuland dry-erase ink in a 50mm Montana case, wrapped with cohesive flexible elastic to help secure my grip. 2015.

Figure 21: *More Joy.* Custom mixed Neuland dry-erase ink that ended up matching
a leaf I had in mind and then found on the floor while drawing. 2015.

Figure 22: *Level One Scribing.* "Lightning Talks" consist of a series of three-minute bursts of content, where it's most important to accurately track data. Colored and digitized in Adobe Photoshop. Permanent ink on foam board, 40"h x 60"w, 2015.

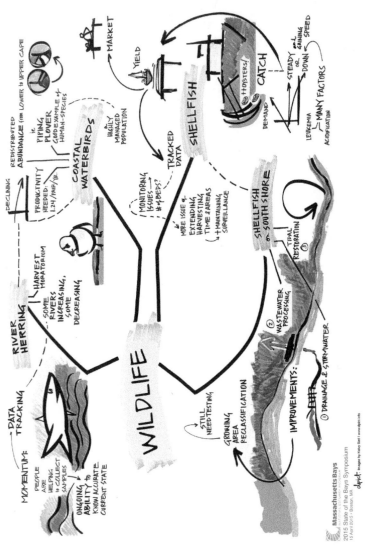

Figure 23: *Level Two Scribing.* Multiple presentations on the topic of wildlife, for a State of the Bays Symposium with Massachusetts Bays National Estuary Program. Permanent ink on foam board, 40"h x 60"w, 2015.

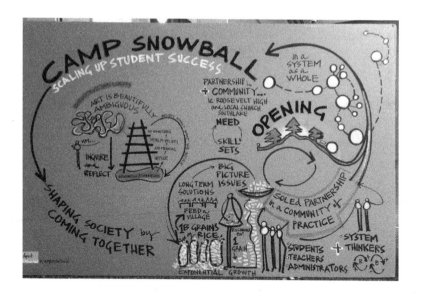

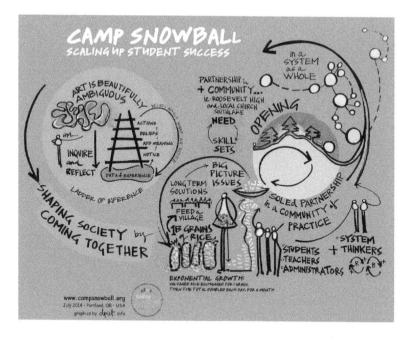

Figure 24: *Level Three Scribing.* This is an example of contextually and visually relating elements, where multiple speakers set the intent for a week-long program. The top image is the "raw" photograph, and tthe bottom is the digitally enhanced file. Portland, OR, USA. Permanent ink and acrylic paint on cardboard, 4'h x 6'w, 2014. www.academyforchange.org.

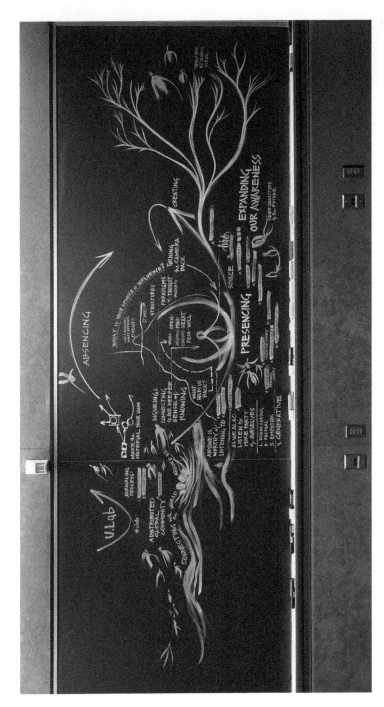

Figure 25: *Level Four Scribing.* Example from u.lab 90-minute session, broadcast live to about 8,000 people from Cambridge, MA, USA. I had multiple chalks and inks ready, but only needed to use one brush and two markers. Chalk ink on blackboard, 5'h x 10'w, 2016.

Figure 26: *Setup.* An example of a container in the room that infused the drawing with a certain quality of care. See the paper on the far right. I sat with the group in the circle until moved to draw, at which point I would rise and work on the wall. Photo credit: Daniel Contrucci.

Figure 27: *Setup.* For the drawing in Figure 28, I hung the paper the evening before the session started, and sat with it a while, deciding how to handle the creases. I let them be, a sign of some kind of freedom.

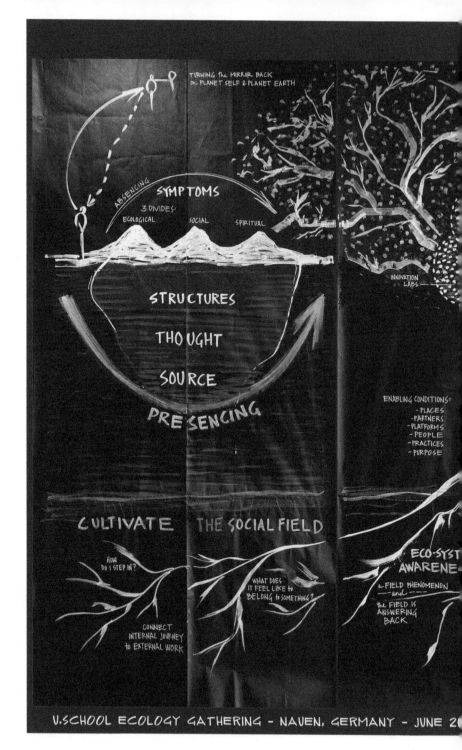

TURNING the MIRROR BACK
on PLANET SELF & PLANET EARTH

SYMPTOMS

ABSENCING

3 DIVIDES:
ECOLOGICAL   SOCIAL   SPIRITUAL

INNOVATION
LABS

STRUCTURES

THOUGHT

SOURCE

PRESENCING

ENABLING CONDITIONS:
- PLACES
- PARTNERS
- PLATFORMS
- PEOPLE
- PRACTICES
- PURPOSE

CULTIVATE   THE SOCIAL FIELD

ECO-SYST
AWARENE

HOW
DO I STEP IN?

WHAT DOES
IT FEEL LIKE to
BELONG to SOMETHING?

a FIELD PHENOMENON
— and —
the FIELD IS
ANSWERING
BACK

CONNECT
INTERNAL JOURNEY
to EXTERNAL WORK

U.SCHOOL ECOLOGY GATHERING - NAUEN, GERMANY - JUNE 2

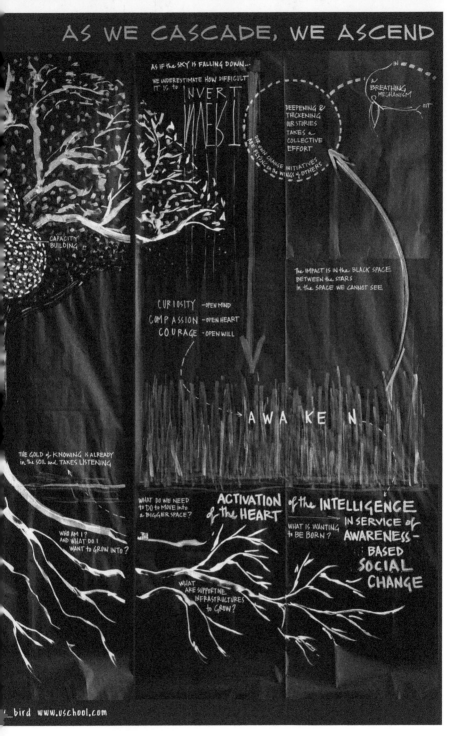

Figure 28: *Generative Scribing.* u.school Ecology. Example of three uses of time and of generative scribing, from a two-day session with about thirty people, in Nauen, Germany. Acrylic paint on paper, 9'h x 12'w, 2016.

Figure 29: *Removal.* The careful removal of the artifact from the wall, after digital documentation.

Figure 30: *Distribution.* I refolded the drawing into sections, for different parts of the system (China, Scotland, and Brazil) to take back to their local hubs.

Figure 31: *Trust.* Detail from Figure 28, and an example of trusting that I would capture the pieces that needed to be seen together. "Invert" became a key theme of the drawing.

Figure 32: *Reflecting.* A client takes a moment to review visual output. 2013.

Figure 33: *Learning.* These drawings (one-third of the complete drawing, which wrapped around the entire room) helped a group track key concepts over five intensive days of learning at an Executive Education program. Dry-erase ink on whiteboard, 4'h x ~28'w, 2014.